July 20

Dear Lou + Deb:

You have no idea how much Gail and I appreciate your friendship.

Your love of our sport and its history are beyond words, and my respect for you is huge.

I hope you enjoy this story

Michael Veitch

SUMMIT OF CHAMPIONS
*Thoroughbred Racing in Saratoga Springs
1901 – 1955*

By Michael Veitch
Edited by Gale Y. Brinkman

∼

Printed by
Advantage Press
74 Warren Street
Saratoga Springs, NY 12866

ISBN: 978-0-63965-0-5
Library of Congress Control Number: 2013905470

Copyright 2013 by Michael Veitch

Cover art: by Anthony P. Farone, Jr.

TABLE OF CONTENTS

Introduction .... p.   3

Giants of the Young Century 1901-1910 .... p.   7

Blackout 1911-1912 .... p. 21

Restoration and a Golden Age of Racing 1913-1939 .... p. 31

Pari-Mutuels Arrive and World War II 1940-1945 .... p. 71

Return to Saratoga and a New Order for the Future .... p. 83

Appendix A. Racing Dates... p. 109

Appendix B. Trivia .... p. 113

Appendix C. Stakes Histories .... p. 115

Appendix D. Chronology.. p. 163

Notes .... p. 169

Selected Bibliography .... p. 175

Acknowledgements and Credits....................................... p. 179

About the Author .... Inside Cover

THE SARATOGA ASSOCIATION
FOR THE IMPROVEMENT OF THE BREED OF HORSES
6 AND 8 EAST 46TH STREET
NEW YORK

INTRODUCTION

This book is a sequel to *Foundations of Fame: Nineteenth Century Thoroughbred Racing in Saratoga Springs*, which covers the years 1863-1900. In that publication, I reviewed the work of the founders of America's oldest extant thoroughbred track. From the beginning, which occurred during the Civil War, Saratoga attracted the nation's leading owners and trainers, establishing the reputation for quality that has been the hallmark of Saratoga throughout its history.

The Saratoga Association for the Improvement of the Breed of Horses was formed in 1865 and guided the track until it was replaced by the Greater New York Association (later the New York Racing Association) in late 1955. This book covers the 20th century history of the Saratoga Association and its ownership of Saratoga Race Course, a period marked by champions like Regret, Man o' War, Exterminator, Equipoise, Top Flight, Tom Fool and Native Dancer.

Saratoga racing during this era, as it had in the 19th century, survived major challenges like the statewide ban on gambling that caused a cessation of racing in 1911 and 1912, and the shifting of race dates to Belmont Park from 1943 through 1945 during World

War II.

The final years of the 19th century had not been the brightest for thoroughbred racing in Saratoga Springs. Begun with such promise at the four-day meeting in 1863 at the old trotting track, the Saratoga summer racing season blossomed quickly into one of national importance. After just two years, the Saratoga races were being compared with those at the famous English courses of Goodwood and Royal Ascot.

Leading American owners such as August Belmont, Leonard Jerome, David McDaniel, Francis Morris, Stephen Sanford, William Cottrill, E.J. "Lucky" Baldwin, James R. Keene, and others raced their top runners at Saratoga Race Course over the next 25 years. Great horses such as Ruthless, Harry Bassett, Duke of Magenta, Miss Woodford, Kentucky, Luke Blackburn, Emperor of Norfolk, Longfellow, and Hindoo won prestigious Saratoga events such as the Alabama, Saratoga Cup, Travers and United States Hotel Stakes. By 1882, the Saratoga meeting was 40 days in length, and the track grounds and stable areas had grown correspondingly. Several owners, who raced with breed improvement and sport as goals, built private stables at Saratoga Race Course.

A gradual weakening of Saratoga racing began in 1891, when Gottfried Walbaum, a part owner of Guttenberg Race Track in

THE SARATOGA ASSOCIATION
FOR THE IMPROVEMENT OF THE BREED OF HORSES
6 AND 8 EAST 46TH STREET
NEW YORK

New Jersey, acquired control of the Saratoga Association. Walbaum, an avid gambler, built a new 5,000-seat grandstand for the 1892 meeting along with other innovations. He claimed in his memoirs, for instance, to have originated the post parade at the 1892 meeting, although there was a post parade for the 1880 Belmont Stakes at Jerome Park. As the 1890's progressed, purses at Saratoga declined under Walbaum's ownership. He also tinkered with post times at the track for various reasons, which displeased local residents.

Finally, Saratoga Race Course hit bottom in 1896 when there was no racing at the famed Union Avenue track. Premier events like the Alabama, Spinaway, and Travers were disrupted during Walbaum's tenure in the 1890's. The Alabama was not run from 1893 through 1896 nor from 1898 through 1900. The Spinaway was not run from 1892 through 1900, while the Travers was not run from 1898 through 1900.

There were some bright spots, though, such as Henry of Navarre winning the Travers in 1894. Hamburg won the Flash Stakes, under 129 pounds, and the Congress Hall Stakes, under 134 pounds, as a two-year-old at the 1897 meeting.

Walbaum's last year of Saratoga Race Course ownership was 1900, a meeting of just 22 days, the same as 1897 and the shortest since the 21-day meeting of 1877. Some owners at the time viewed

Saratoga as a place to merely freshen their horses for the fall meetings at downstate tracks in the New York metropolitan area and on Long Island. The idea of building a new track was entertained by some citizens of Saratoga Springs as a way to deal with Walbaum.

With a new century at hand, the future of Saratoga Race Course was secured when the great sportsman William C. Whitney and a syndicate purchased the track in late 1900. His partners included top owners John Sanford, Perry Belmont and P. J. Dwyer. His vision for Saratoga thoroughbred racing would restore the track to its former status, and ensure its future.

Chapter I
GIANTS OF THE YOUNG CENTURY
1901-1910

THE WHITNEY REVIVAL

With William C. Whitney as president of the Saratoga Association, there were high hopes in racing circles that the 1901 season would mark a return of top class sport to the Spa. Several new stakes races, including the Adirondack, Saratoga Special, and Saratoga Handicap were inaugurated in 1901. As opening day Monday, August 5, neared, track stables overflowed with horses preparing for the 22-day meeting.

The Saratoga Handicap was described in the *New York Times* as an addition to the prestigious and older Brooklyn and Suburban handicaps as a top eastern event.[1] The winner's value of $6,800 compared favorably to the $7,800 in both the Brooklyn, inaugurated in 1887, and the Suburban, inaugurated in 1884. The Adirondack was open to both sexes prior to 1930, and there was more than a little irony for its first edition on August 24. The winner was Smart Set, owned by Gottfried Walbaum. The Saratoga Special was established as a winner-take-all race for two-year-olds and was captured on

August 10 by Goldsmith, owned by Whitney. The race remained a winner-take-all event until 1959.

The Travers Stakes (which had not been run since 1897) was renewed on August 10 and won by Blues, who collected $6,750, a figure that reflected the investment and spirit of the new Whitney era. The 1897 winner was Rensselaer, who earned $1,425. Blues was one of the stars of the 1901 meeting. In addition to the Travers Stakes he also won the Delaware Handicap on August 17 and the famed Saratoga Cup on August 24. Inaugurated in 1865, the Saratoga Cup was one of the oldest races in North America, predated only by the Phoenix Handicap (1831), Queen's Plate (1860), and Travers Stakes (1864).

Having positioned Saratoga Race Course for a healthy future, Whitney went on to enjoy a terrific year on the American turf. He was the leading owner in 1901 with stable earnings of $108,400, a title he would also win in 1903 with $102,569. Late in the year, the *Saratogian* reported that Whitney's plans for 1902 included lengthening the main track from one mile to one and one-eighth miles. The track in 1902 also included a turf course for flat racing and an inner turf course for steeplechase racing.[2]

The Sanford family of Amsterdam, racing at Saratoga Race Course since the 1870's, also enjoyed outstanding success during the early years of the 20th century. Gen. Stephen Sanford, born in 1826, was the builder of Hurricana Stud in Amsterdam, about 25 miles west of Saratoga Springs. The Sanfords bred and raised their horses at Hurricana Stud, and pointed them for the annual Saratoga meeting each summer, racing them in their purple and gold silks.

Sanford runners held their own, and then some, against powerful downstate outfits belonging to Harry Payne Whitney, Richard T. Wilson, John E. Madden, James R. Keene, and others who were racing at the metropolitan New York meetings before the Saratoga season. Leading horses of this time carrying the Sanford colors included Caughnawaga, Chuctununda, Molly Brant, Mohawk II, Kennyetto, Sir John Johnson and Herkimer.

The Sanford runner Molly Brant won the Adirondack Stakes at the Spa in 1902, beginning quite a run of stakes victories at the track. She won the Saranac Stakes in 1903, and in 1904 captured three stakes races, topped by a victory over Travers winner Broomstick in the Merchants' and Citizens' Handicap. Molly Brant also won the Delaware Handicap and Champlain Handicap in 1904. Her greatest victory came in the Delaware Handicap of 1905, in which she defeated Beldame and Roseben, both future Hall of Fame horses.

A few days after the Delaware Handicap in 1905, Mohawk II, perhaps the best runner bred by the Sanfords, won the Hopeful Stakes

THE SARATOGA ASSOCIATION
FOR THE IMPROVEMENT OF THE BREED OF HORSES
6 AND 8 EAST 46TH STREET
NEW YORK

The mausoleum and family plot of Stephen Sanford at Green Hill Cemetery in Amsterdam, N.Y.

under 130 pounds. A half-brother to the Sanford's Caughnawaga, winner of the Saratoga Handicap and Saratoga Cup in 1905, Mohawk II was unveiled at the famous Sanford Matinee, the hugely popular day of trial racing and celebration hosted by the Sanfords at Hurricana each year a few weeks before the opening of the Saratoga season. His Hopeful victory, though, came with a price, for Mohawk II was discovered to have suffered a stone bruise.

Mohawk II endured several years of bad luck following the Hopeful, his final start of 1905. At the Sanford Matinee of 1906, he appeared in a trial race and finished third, cheered on by a crowd estimated at 15,000-20,000.[3] Mohawk II made it to the Travers Stakes that summer and finished second to Gallavant. A skin disease kept him out of action for all of 1907. He made an appearance at the Sanford Matinee of 1908 and lost to the younger filly Donascara at one mile. Mohawk II made his final career start that summer in the Saratoga Handicap on opening day. He broke down in the stretch while leading the field and was retired to stud.

Hurricana Stud was the leading owner at Saratoga in 1905, with earnings of $47,090 which bettered the totals of the Keene and Whitney stables.[4] Along with Mohawk II, one of the big Sanford earners was Caughnawaga, who captured the Saratoga Handicap and Saratoga Cup, in each case defeating the great Beldame.

THE SARATOGA ASSOCIATION
FOR THE IMPROVEMENT OF THE BREED OF HORSES
6 AND 8 EAST 46TH STREET
NEW YORK

At Saratoga in 1907, Kennyetto won the Alabama Stakes and Huron Stakes, defeating males in the latter. In some polls, she was named champion three-year-old filly. At the same meeting, the Sanford filly Vails won the Delaware Handicap over older runners, getting the mile in a sharp 1:38, and later defeated males in the Saranac Handicap. During the next three seasons, Sanford victories continued with Sir John Johnson, Mayfield, Rockville, Donascara and others.

In 1910, the last year of racing before a two-year blackout of the sport in New York, Stephen Sanford was 84 years old. In the midst of a fight along with other leaders of the turf to prevent the shutdown, he won nine races at that Saratoga meeting. He could not have known it at the time, but the General was watching his beloved runners in purple and gold compete for the last time at Saratoga Race Course. The stable raced at Blue Bonnets in Montreal, in 1911, with some success. However, he took ill in late 1912 and died on February 13, 1913, a few months before the return of racing at Saratoga.

Another great, William C. Whitney, died on February 2, 1904, in New York City at age 62. He had just begun a fascination with thoroughbred breeding, and made an impact that continues to our time. In 1902 he published *The Whitney Stud,* a book of nearly 600 pages that detailed the pedigree and racing history of the bloodstock he had acquired.

In volume one of his book, *Legacies of the Turf — A Century of Great Thoroughbred Breeders,* racing historian Ed Bowen lists four champions bred by Whitney during the short time he was active in this aspect of the sport. One was Tanya, a foal of 1902 by Meddler, purchased by Whitney for $49,000.[5] Meddler raced only as a two-year-old in England, winning all three starts in 1892. Tanya's mother was Handspun, a daughter of the great Hall of Fame filly Spinaway, for whom the ancient Saratoga stakes race is named. The Spinaway is the oldest stakes race in the United States for two-year-old fillies. Tanya was one of several high class runners that made the 1904 season at the Spa a truly memorable one.

She won the 15th edition of the Spinaway Stakes on August 3, and on August 13 she won the prestigious Hopeful Stakes over males under top weight of 127 pounds, conceding ten rivals from five to 15 pounds. Tanya is the only winner of both events at Saratoga. Bee Mac won both events at Belmont Park in 1943, when the Saratoga races were contested downstate. In 1905, Tanya became the second of only three fillies to win the Belmont Stakes, the first being Ruthless in the inaugural edition of the race in 1867. Rags to Riches became the third in 2007.

James R. Keene's top two-year-old Sysonby was at Saratoga in

1904 and won the Flash Stakes on opening day. He also won the Saratoga Special, and went on to win 14 of 15 starts in his career, losing only the Futurity Stakes at Sheepshead Bay as the heavy favorite. Sysonby was reported drugged before the race.[6] Elected to the Hall of Fame in 1956, Sysonby deadheated for the Metropolitan Handicap in his first start as a three-year-old, and added important events such as the Lawrence Realization at Sheepshead Bay and Great Republic at Saratoga that year.

The Flash, inaugurated in 1869, was one of the oldest races in the United States. It was restored in 1902 by Whitney and the new management, not having been run in 1896, 1898, 1899 or 1900. The five and one-half furlong race for two-year-olds enjoyed quite a reputation among horsemen, and it's easy to see why. In addition to Sysonby, two more Hall of Fame horses soon won the Flash; Peter Pan in 1906 and Fair Play in 1907. Old Rosebud, yet another Hall of Famer, won the Flash in 1913. During 1901-1955, seven Hall of Fame horses won the race, with Gallant Fox (1929), Assault (1945) and Native Dancer (1952) joining the aforementioned quartet of Sysonby, Peter Pan, Fair Play and Old Rosebud. Gallant Fox and Assault won the Triple Crown the following season as three-year-olds, respectively, in 1930 and 1946.

Still another great runner at the 22-day Saratoga meeting in 1904 was Beldame, who won the Alabama Stakes as she pleased over just two other sophomore fillies, and followed with the historic Saratoga Cup at a mile and three-quarters in the slop over males. Owned by August Belmont II, Beldame was considered America's best horse overall and champion three-year-old filly in 1904.[7] She went on to win the Suburban Handicap as a four-year-old, and retired with earnings of $102,135, joining Miss Woodford and Firenze as the only fillies up to that time to earn more than $100,000. Beldame was elected to the Hall of Fame in 1956.

A third Hall of Fame horse to have raced at Saratoga in 1904 was Broomstick, who was elected along with Beldame in 1956. Owned by Capt. Samuel S. Brown, he won the Travers Stakes that year over moderate opposition. Prior to the Saratoga meeting that year, he won the Brighton Handicap in an American record of 2:02 4/5 for a mile and a quarter. That mark stood until his son, Whisk Broom II, broke it in 1913 in the Suburban Handicap.

Regarding Whisk Broom II, in 1913 he became the first of only four winners of the old and fabled New York handicap triple crown, consisting of the Metropolitan, Brooklyn and Suburban handicaps. The Suburban was inaugurated in 1884, the Brooklyn in 1887, and the Metropolitan in 1891. Whisk Broom II was followed by Tom Fool (1953), Kelso (1961), and Fit to Fight (1984) as winners of the triple.

Following the death of William C. Whitney, Francis R. Hitchcock became president of the Saratoga Association. The first meeting he presided over was the 22-day season of 1905. The Saratogian reported a week before opening day that the 2,800 stalls on the grounds of the track were full, and that applications exceeded availability. Grandstand admission was $3, while $1 would get a racing fan into the infield for the races.[8]

Among the highlights of the 1905 season was the victory of Sysonby in the $50,000 Great Republic Stakes on August 12, with some 20,000 in attendance. Roseben, another Hall of Famer, made only two of his 111 career starts at Saratoga, and both came at this meeting. On August 22 he won a handicap at six furlongs under 140 pounds. During seven seasons of racing, Roseben won 52 races.

Race cards with multiple stakes events were frequently conducted by the Saratoga Association during this era. The 1906 meeting opened on August 6 with three stakes: the $10,000 Saratoga Handicap, the $6,000 Flash Stakes, and the $5,000 Saratoga Steeplechase. James R. Keene's Peter Pan won the Flash under 125 pounds and the Hopeful Stakes under 130 pounds at this stand. The following year, Peter Pan won the Belmont Stakes and other important New York races. He retired with 10 wins in 17 starts and earnings of $115,450 in two seasons of racing.

The short-lived experiment of a Derby at Saratoga ended in 1906. Begun in 1904, with a purse of $5,000, the inaugural was won by Keene's good runner Delhi, who also that year at Saratoga won the $50,000 Great Republic Stakes. Delhi, who did not run in the Kentucky Derby, won the Belmont Stakes, and was considered the champion three-year-old along with Ort Wells.[9]

The filly Maskette, elected to the Hall of Fame in 2001, was born in 1906. Bred and owned by Keene, she won 12 of 17 starts, including two of the most important for her sex at Saratoga. After breaking her maiden on August 3, 1908, at the Spa, she won the Spinaway Stakes with ease just two days later, racing five and one-half furlongs in 1:05 4/5, or four-fifths faster than her debut time of 1:06 3/5. Maskette went on to win five of six starts as a juvenile filly, defeating males in the Futurity and concluding her season with a win in the Matron Stakes. Maskette returned to Saratoga to capture the Alabama Stakes in 1909, despite having to overcome the sloppy going.

As the magnificent Personal Ensign marched through her glorious unbeaten career during 1986-1988, winning 13 races, she was often compared to Colin, still another from the stable of James. R. Keene. Colin appeared as a two-year-old at Saratoga in 1907, winning the

Saratoga Special on August 10 and the Grand Union Hotel on August 14. Yet another Hall of Famer to race at Saratoga during this period, Colin went on to win all 15 of his races. Twelve came as a juvenile, as he sped through a season virtually unchallenged at the New York tracks. He returned as a three-year-old to win the Withers, Belmont and Tidal to wrap up his career. Colin was considered America's best horse in both seasons he raced.

During this period Keene's stable won a remarkable number of important stakes. He won the Hopeful with Delhi in 1903 and Helmet in 1908. In addition to Maskette's victory, he also won the Spinaway with Duster in 1902 and Court Dress in 1906. He posted scores in the United States Hotel with Restigouche (1907), Hilarious (1908) and Grasmere (1909). Hilarious returned in 1909 to win the Travers Stakes for Keene. The stable also scored victories in the Seneca, Mohawk, Kenner, Troy, and Grand Union Hotel, and Great Republic.

To have seen the likes of Mohawk II, Tanya, Beldame, Sysonby, Colin, Fair Play, Beldame, Maskette and Peter Pan during the early years of the new century was to have experienced some of the very finest in thoroughbred racing. There were, however, developments brewing that would again threaten Saratoga racing, much as they had in the 1890's during the Walbaum era.

THE SARATOGA ASSOCIATION
FOR THE IMPROVEMENT OF THE BREED OF HORSES
6 AND 8 EAST 46TH STREET
NEW YORK

Anti-gambling sentiments had been strengthening during the reform era of Progressives in the late 19th and early 20th centuries. In 1908, the Hart-Agnew law prohibited betting and had an immediate impact on Saratoga racing. The season that year was but 15 days in length, the shortest since the 14-day meeting in 1876. An odd loophole in Hart-Agnew permitted oral wagering, but not the open bookmaking that gamblers preferred. The *Saratogian* noted that opening day, July 30, was marked by the presence of police officers at the track, making sure Hart-Agnew was enforced.[10]

But Saratoga Springs and New York racing were in trouble, as all state tracks lost money in 1908 and the bloodstock business was marked by falling prices. A number of leading American owners began to race in England, France, and Canada.

The 24-day season at Saratoga in 1910 completed a run of 14 years following the shutdown of 1896. However, it would be followed by a two-year blackout in 1911 and 1912 because of anti-gambling statutes. The Jockey Club announced the New York season would conclude with Saratoga, and to that end transferred the Futurity Stakes to the Spa from Sheepshead Bay. It was run on August 31 and captured by Sam Hildreth's champion juvenile Novelty, who also won the Saratoga Special and Hopeful Stakes. The Alabama went to a good one that year, too, as Woodford Clay's Ocean Bound won it on the way to three-year-old filly championship honors.

It was a summer at Saratoga dripping with racing history. John Hunter, who had helped organize the first meetings at Horse Haven in 1863 and whose horse Kentucky won the inaugural Travers Stakes in 1864, made an appearance at the track and received applause from the crowd. Hunter was invited to preside with the other stewards for the running of the Saratoga Special on August 13. Four days later, Novelty defeated Textile in a match race, worth $5,000 a side, by three lengths in 1:13 1/5 for six furlongs. And Stephen Sanford, who would not live to see Saratoga racing resume in 1913, was honored with the inauguration of the Hurricana Stakes, named in honor of his farm in Amsterdam.

Chapter II
BLACKOUT 1911-1912

THE ANTI-GAMBLING IMPACT

For the second time in its history, there was no racing at Saratoga Race Course in 1911 and 1912. The first was in 1896, a season lost following several years of disenchantment with the track's former principal owner, Gottfried Walbaum. The situation was similar in the years preceding the second shutdown.

The United States was in the midst of a general spirit of reform at this time, referred to in history textbooks as the Progressive Era. Progressives worked to better society through the enfranchisement of greater numbers of voters, the improvement of working conditions in the industrial age, and the expansion of civil rights. Gambling – and that meant racing – did not escape their attention as a social problem in need of reform.

Many states had joined New York in the revival of racing after the Civil War. There were hundreds of tracks in the late 19th century, a number that began to shrink rapidly in the early years of the 20th century. Stories about race-fixing led to numerous anti-gambling laws. The one that eventually closed New York tracks was the Hart-Agnew legislation of 1908.

Goodwin's Turf Guide, in its annual review of racing, noted in the Saratoga section: "Being contrary to law, there was no public betting."[1] The legislation prohibited open gambling and bookmaking, but made provisions for betting in other ways. For example, those who wished to wager on a race had to whisper the selection to a bookmaker, who was not able to record it in the usual manner of writing it down on a ledger. This system made it impossible for bookmakers, relying on memory, to handle the normal volume of wagers.

With Hart-Agnew in place, the seasons of 1908, 1909, and 1910, while marked by some fine sport, saw a general downturn of business, especially at the New York City tracks. Saratoga, with its national reputation as a summer place, fared better than the downstate tracks. Still, the Spa had to deal not only with Hart-Agnew, but the threat of Empire City track in Yonkers.

Empire City had opened in 1900 with the intention of being a trotting track. However, it conducted a thoroughbred meeting in 1907 in competition with Saratoga. Since most of the leading eastern stables were already at Saratoga Race Course, Empire City's meeting drew support from other parts of the country. When The Jockey Club recognized Empire City in 1908, a calendar conflict arose with Saratoga Race Course. Only 11 days were proposed at Saratoga, from

July 30 to August 11, while the schedule proposed for Empire City was for August 12 to August 28. The Saratoga meeting had been cut in half. With Stephen Sanford taking the lead, an accommodation was reached between the officials of both tracks, and Saratoga got an additional four days.

On opening day at Saratoga, July 30, 1908, policemen were on hand to enforce Hart-Agnew. Betting took place in hushed tones and newspaper accounts of the meeting regularly carried reports of the enforcement of the law. The season, though, was not a strong one financially for the Saratoga Association. It reported a loss of $30,000, a situation aggravated by Empire City. The association said it would look for a restoration of its former dates for 1909.

New York Governor Charles Evans Hughes, in attendance at the Ballston County Fair on August 26, 1908, tried to assure Saratogians that the Hart-Agnew law would not hurt their summer business. While saying he understood their fears about the racing industry, Gov. Hughes pointed to the mineral springs as a way for Saratoga to restore its fame. The *Saratogian* reported that angry horsemen at the fair snubbed the state's chief executive, and refused to conduct horse races in his presence. Despite management's urging to the horsemen to conduct the races, they waited until Gov. Hughes left the fair to catch a 4 p.m. train.[2]

In late 1908, the oral betting provision of the Hart-Agnew law was upheld unanimously by the five judges of the Appellate Division of the Supreme Court of New York State. The court ruled that Hart-Agnew was aimed at bookmakers and the selling of pools, not at private wagers. The decision was upheld by the New York State Court of Appeals in 1909.

Still, this ruling did not please the Anti-Race Track Gambling Campaign Committee, whose members compiled a list of complaints about continued gambling excesses at the Saratoga meeting in 1908. Among them were continued record-keeping of bets, money being passed openly in betting activity, and the presence of bookmakers on the grounds.[3]

The end of gambling and racing came with the passage of the Directors Criminal Liability Act in 1910. The law held the owners of New York tracks criminally liable for violations of anti-gambling statutes. It was passed in September and resulted in the cancellation of the fall race meetings in the state, originally slated to end on November 15. The situation was a stomach punch to American and New York racing.

Many owners had already been sending horses to England and France for a few years, as the anti-gambling forces gained steam in the early years of the 20th century. For example, Harry Payne Whitney, the son of William C. Whitney, sent Whisk Broom II to England as a yearling in 1908, where the Hall of Fame runner made his first 23 starts. When racing resumed in New York on May 30, 1913, Whisk Broom II was among the American horses that returned and on that day he won the Metropolitan Handicap. He made just two more starts and won them both, the Brooklyn Handicap on June 21 and the Suburban Handicap on June 28, thus becoming the first winner of the old New York handicap triple crown. Other top horses of the era that were sent overseas included Artful, Tanya, Maskette and Peter Pan.

With the racing scene in turmoil, the nation's bloodstock prices fell. The average price for a yearling in 1909 was $412, with $284,845 spent at the auction sales. In 1911, the average was $226, with only $87,957 spent at auction.[4] The average purse per race suffered a similar decline. It was $736.58 in 1908, but only $371.75 in 1911.[5]

In early 1911, The Jockey Club, not willing to test the Directors Criminal Liability Act, announced there would be no racing at its tracks. The Saratoga Association had hoped to conduct a meeting that summer, but went along with the decision, ushering in two enigmatic summers at the Spa. Despite the ban in New York, Saratogian Frank Nolan, the owner of Beverwyck Stable, brought his horses to Saratoga in the summer of 1912 and then had them conditioned at the Oklahoma Training Track by trainer David Woodford.

Following The Jockey Club decision, the Sanford Stable, so long prominent and popular at Saratoga Race Course, sold its horses of racing age. The sale took pace at Kenilworth Park in Ontario on August 3, with 22 horses fetching $30,025. One of the buyers was leading Canadian owner Joseph E. Seagram, who purchased Sanford's horse Rockville for $5,200. Rockville raced in Seagram's colors at Blue Bonnets Race Track in Montreal.

Horses belonging to stables like those of Saratoga Association president Richard T. Wilson, August Belmont II, and Harry Payne Whitney began appearing in the entries at the Fort Erie, Windsor and Hamilton tracks in Canada. Wilson's fine runner Olambala, winner of the Suburban Handicap and Saratoga Handicap in 1910, was racing at Fort Erie and other Canadian tracks in 1911 and 1912.

Wilson visited Saratoga Race Course in August, 1911, where some 250 horses were in training and the grounds were open to the public. According to the *Schenectady Evening Star*, a popular activity with fans was the schooling of jumping horses each morning. President Wilson expressed the hope that the free admission might attract some new fans to Saratoga racing, especially those who were anti-racing and anti-gambling.[6]

THE SARATOGA ASSOCIATION
FOR THE IMPROVEMENT OF THE BREED OF HORSES
6 AND 8 EAST 46TH STREET
NEW YORK

Fort Erie Race Track — Starting a Race.

Fort Erie Race Track in Ontario, where some Saratoga owners raced during 1911 and 1912.

During the summer of 1911, there were hopes that racing would somehow still be held at Saratoga. In July, the Gittens Bill was introduced in the state legislature to relieve track owners of the punishments in the Directors Criminal Liability Act. It failed, although it attracted the support of anti-gambling crusader State Senator Edgar Truman Brackett of Saratoga Springs. The Gittens Bill was acted on several times that month, passing in one house but failing in the other. As it played out that July, horses continued to arrive in Saratoga Springs, their owners hoping for some sort of meeting.

Sen. Brackett, in a letter to the *Saratogian* on July 27, blamed the track owners for the lack of racing. He said, in effect, the directors were overreacting to the Directors Criminal Liability Act. Sen. Brackett noted the law was aimed at professional gamblers and gambling rings, and not the casual fan who might like to place a bet on the races. Sen. Brackett warned that Saratogians might blame the track owners for not thinking of the city's prosperity if it remained closed.[7]

There were small pockets of racing in 1911 that conformed to the law. Harness racing's Grand Circuit was held at Buffalo, and the New York and Parkway Driving Clubs conducted harness and flat racing in New York City for purse money only.

THE SARATOGA ASSOCIATION
FOR THE IMPROVEMENT OF THE BREED OF HORSES
6 AND 8 EAST 46TH STREET
NEW YORK

The state of Maryland benefited from the ban on racing in New York. On August 24, 1912, a new race course, Havre de Grace, opened there with official recognition by The Jockey Club. Its officials included those who had previously worked at Saratoga summer meetings, such as handicapper Walter S. Vosburgh, and judges C. H. Pettengill and C. J. Fitzgerald.

Perhaps most important that year, Supreme Court Justice Townsend Scudder, of Nassau County, made a ruling that led to the return of racing in New York in 1913. It dealt with the case of Paul Shane, accused of violating the anti-gambling laws at a hunt meeting at Belmont in 1912. Justice Scudder held that Shane, making an ordinary bet on a race, was not breaking the law that prohibited organized bookmaking. He also ruled that such bets relieved track directors of responsibility for them, and that directors could not be held responsible for bookmaking activities unless they had full knowledge of them.[8]

In early 1913, the Appellate Division of the Supreme Court in Brooklyn upheld the ruling by Justice Scudder, clearing the way for racing to formally resume on May 30 at Belmont Park. The Saratoga Association would reopen for the track's 48th meeting on August 2.

THE SARATOGA ASSOCIATION
FOR THE IMPROVEMENT OF THE BREED OF HORSES
6 AND 8 EAST 46TH STREET
NEW YORK

Chapter III
RESTORATION AND A GOLDEN AGE OF RACING 1913-1939

RACING RETURNS TO SARATOGA

The stables of leading owners H. P. Whitney, Greentree, E. R. Bradley and others were among those gathering at Saratoga Race Course a few weeks before the resumption of racing at the Spa in 1913. These men and others were in agreement that the track was in good shape despite the two-year shutdown of 1911-1912.

The *Saratogian* reported an opening day crowd of 10,000 on August 2, 1913. Three stakes races, the Shillelah Steeplechase, Flash, and Saratoga Handicap were contested on the first day of the 26-day season. The great Old Rosebud, who had begun his career at Juarez, Mexico on February 9 with a victory at 3 ½ furlongs, won the Flash as the heavy favorite under top weight of 124 pounds. It was his 13th start as a two-year-old and he won as he pleased, conceding 12 pounds to second-place Stromboli. Old Rosebud, a member of the National Museum of Racing Hall of Fame, completed his juvenile season with a victory in the United States Hotel Stakes on August 13. He won 12 of his 13 outings and was the champion of his foal crop of 1911 off that record.

Old Rosebud, bred by John E. Madden, would win 40 of his 80 career starts, racing to age 11 and also winning the Kentucky Derby, Carter Handicap, and other major events. He won the Delaware Handicap at Saratoga in 1917 under 133 pounds, a race in which another Hall of Famer born in 1911, Roamer, finished third under 127 pounds.

Andrew Miller's Roamer won the Saratoga Special in 1913, although his two-year-old season did not compare to Old Rosebud's. He won 12 of 16 races as a three-year-old, with wins in such important events as the Carter and Brooklyn Derby. Back at Saratoga in 1914, Roamer won the Travers by 10 lengths, a margin of victory that stood until it was bettered by General Assembly in 1979. Roamer's margin equaled that of Tom Bowling in 1873 and was also recorded by Ace Admiral in 1948 and Wajima in 1975.

There is no question Roamer loved Saratoga. He won the Huron Handicap following his Travers victory; the Saratoga Handicap, Merchants' and Citizens', and Saratoga Cup in 1915; and the Saratoga Handicap again in 1917 and 1918. In a famous race against time on August 21 at the 1918 Saratoga meeting, Roamer set a new American record of 1:34 4/5 for one mile.

Also at Saratoga for the return of racing in 1913 was the

well-known steeplechase jockey Elliott Wolke, who lived at Saratoga Lake for many years in his retirement. Wolke, in the decade of 1910-1920, was one of the leading steeplechase riders of his time, appearing at all the major meetings in Canada and the eastern United States. Among the stables he rode and worked for were Joseph E. Widener, Brookmeade Stable, Rokeby Stable, Commander J. K. L. Ross, and Richard T. Wilson. In 1915 at Saratoga, aboard the great jumper Weldship, Wolke won the Beverwyck, North American, and Saratoga Steeplechase handicaps.

One who did not make the 1913 season at his beloved Saratoga was Stephen Sanford, who had been racing at Saratoga Race Course since the 1870's. Sanford died on February 13, 1913, at age 86. On August 23 that year, the Saratoga Racing Association inaugurated the Sanford Memorial Stakes in his honor. It is one of the prizes of two-year-old racing at Saratoga, and has been won by many greats, including Hall of Fame horses Regret, Tom Fool, Secretariat, and Affirmed. A Sanford family tradition continued at Saratoga Race Course throughout the 20th century with regard to the race. In what is surely a rare practice at major American tracks, the family continued to privately produce and award the sterling silver cup to the winner of the Sanford Memorial Stakes at Saratoga. John Sanford, the son of Stephen Sanford, began the practice in 1919.[1] The cup was designed by John Darwell in England, during the reign of King George III in 1769. Sanford purchased it, and offered permanent possession to any owner who won three editions, not necessarily consecutive, of the race.

Regret would be the first filly to win the greatest single prize in American racing, the Kentucky Derby. Bred and owned by Harry Payne Whitney, the son of William C. Whitney, she raced three times as a two-year-old of 1914. All came at Saratoga Race Course, and all came in open stakes against the opposite sex. Regret opened her career with a victory as the favorite in the Saratoga Special on August 8, 1914, and defeated the male Pebbles by one length. Her victory was described in the racing charts as "speed in reserve." On August 15 she won the Sanford Memorial by a length and a half under 127 pounds, described as "under restraint throughout."[2]

Her performance in the Hopeful Stakes, on August 22, revealed the nature of Regret's character. She caught a heavy track that day and for the only time in her career was not on the lead in the early stages. Regret, again under 127 pounds, gradually wore down the leaders in the stretch to win by a half-length over Andrew M., to whom she conceded 13 pounds. Three lengths back in third was Pebbles, under 130 pounds.

So, in just 14 days, Regret swept three important Saratoga stakes

THE SARATOGA ASSOCIATION
FOR THE IMPROVEMENT OF THE BREED OF HORSES
6 AND 8 EAST 46TH STREET
NEW YORK

Regret won the Saratoga Special, Sanford Memorial, and Hopeful Stakes in 1914 at Saratoga.

races and was then put on the shelf. She did not appear again until the Kentucky Derby on May 8, 1915, a layoff of an incredible 259 days, off just three races at 6 furlongs. She led all the way to win by two lengths over Pebbles. Her victory in the Kentucky Derby, at 10 furlongs, is considered by racing historians as a milestone in boosting the prestige and popularity of the race.

Regret followed her Kentucky Derby victory with a win in the Saranac Stakes at Saratoga on August 17, running her unbeaten record to five, and all over males. Her season ended that day, and she returned the following year in the Saratoga Handicap on July 31, losing for the first time in her career and finishing eighth, the only race in which she failed to hit the board. She made one more start as a four-year-old, on August 18 in an allowance with an easy victory at one mile.

Regret raced four times as a five-year-old in 1917, losing only the Brooklyn Handicap by a nose to stablemate Borrow while conceding five pounds. As per custom, she led throughout and was caught at the wire by Borrow. She was a length better than Old Rosebud while conceding two pounds. This edition of the Brooklyn was a corker, and also included Omar Khayyam, winner of that year's Kentucky Derby, and Roamer. Both Old Rosebud, winner of the Kentucky Derby in 1914, and Roamer are members of the Hall of Fame.

She won her final two career starts after the Brooklyn, both in easy fashion. Regret won the Gazelle Handicap over females on July 10, and an open handicap over just one other opponent on September 25 at Aqueduct. She retired with a record of 9-1-0 in 11 starts and earnings of $35,093, having won five races at Saratoga.

Regret was bred, like so many in generations of Whitney breeding, to be top class. She was born at Whitney's Brookdale Farm in Red Bank, New Jersey. Her sire, Broomstick, won the Travers Stakes in 1904 and was America's leading sire in 1913, 1914, and 1915. When Regret was a yearling in 1913, Broomstick's son Whisk Broom II won the famous New York handicap triple crown, consisting of the Metropolitan, Brooklyn and Suburban handicaps. Her mother was Jersey Lightning, whose grandmother Modesty defeated males in the American Derby of 1884. Jersey Lightning also produced Regret's full brother Thunderer, winner of the prestigious Futurity Stakes in 1915. Jersey Lightning's sire was Hamburg, a member of the Hall of Fame who captured the Congress Hall Stakes at Saratoga under 134 pounds in 1897 and ended his career with a 100-length victory at Brighton Beach in the Brighton Cup at two and one-quarter miles.

This was an exciting and promising period for Saratoga racing. At the conclusion of the 1916 season, the *New York Times* reviewed the renewed health of the city and its activities. Recalling the pre-Civil War era of resort prestige and popularity, it said the city "has come back into her own." The article listed the strong stables supporting racing, the mineral springs, and the travel restrictions of World War I as major factors. On the last item, the newspaper said wealthy tourists had curtailed their trips to Europe, with Saratoga the recipient of their expenditures at the time.[3]

In 1917, the Fasig-Tipton Company conducted its first yearling sale in Saratoga Springs during the racing season. The idea of selling at Saratoga was yet another idea favored by William C. Whitney during his investments in the track following his purchase in 1900. He did not live to see it, but his reasoning that there could no better place for selling top yearlings was on the mark. With many leading owners racing at the Spa, he figured they would shop there for future racing prospects.[4] Ever since, the Saratoga Summer Yearling Sale has been one of the nation's most popular and productive venues.

Fasig-Tipton also sponsored The Sales Stakes, which was inaugurated in 1922 at Saratoga. The company donated a $500 silver cup to the owner of the winner of the event, held for two-year-olds sold the previous year at its Saratoga auction. The race was at 5 ½ furlongs, and was contested for several decades.

At the end of 1917, the Saratoga Association announced it would spend $100,000 on improvements to the track. One improvement was a new main track for the 1918 meeting. Some two feet of soil and clay were taken from a large section of land inside the track for the project, the result of which was the creation of the infield lake.

The new track produced terrific clockings. As noted earlier, Roamer raced a mile in 1:34 4/5 against time on August 21. Two racing immortals, Sir Barton and Man o' War, turned in spectacular times for a mile and one-quarter as the decade of the 1920's got underway at Saratoga.

On August 2, opening day of the 1920 season, Sir Barton won the Saratoga Handicap in 2:01 4/5 for the distance, a new track record for a mile and one-quarter. Finishing second by two lengths that day was the great Exterminator, who received three pounds from Sir Barton. First winner of the United States Triple Crown in 1919, Sir Barton had a totally forgettable two-year-old season at the Spa in 1918. In the Flash he was ninth, beaten 15 ½ lengths; in the United States Hotel he was ninth, beaten 16 lengths; in the Sanford Memorial he was seventh, beaten 19 lengths, and in the Hopeful he finished 16th of 20 starters. Sir Barton did not race at Saratoga during 1919, but returned as a four-year-old in 1920 to add the Merchants' and Citizens' Handicap to his victory in the Saratoga Handicap.

Man o' War equaled Sir Barton's record in the Travers Stakes, run on August 21 before a crowd estimated at 30,000, including 5,000 in the infield. His Travers mark lasted for 42 years, until Jaipur won the 1962 edition in 2:01 3/5 in his epic battle with Ridan, one of the truly great races in Saratoga history. Man o' War loved Saratoga, although he lost the only race of his career of 21 starts in the Sanford Memorial of 1919 to Upset. At the Spa, Man o' War won the United States, Grand Union and Hopeful stakes in 1919, and followed with the Miller and Travers stakes in 1920.

The Rancocas Stable dominated the 1922 season at Saratoga. With origins going back to Pierre Lorillard in the late 19th century, it was owned by Harry F. Sinclair at the time. While Rancocas had been a major force in racing for decades, its record in 1922 at the Spa was extraordinary.

With trainer Sam Hildreth conditioning its runners, Grey Lag won the Saratoga Handicap on opening day, August 1. In the following 26 days, Hildreth saddled the winners of 14 more named races. Topping the list were Edict in the Schuylerville and Spinaway, Mad Hatter in the Champlain, Little Chief in the Saranc and Travers, and Zev in the Albany and Grand Union Hotel.

GREAT PATRONS OF THE SPORT AT SARATOGA

For most of its history, Saratoga Race Course has been marked

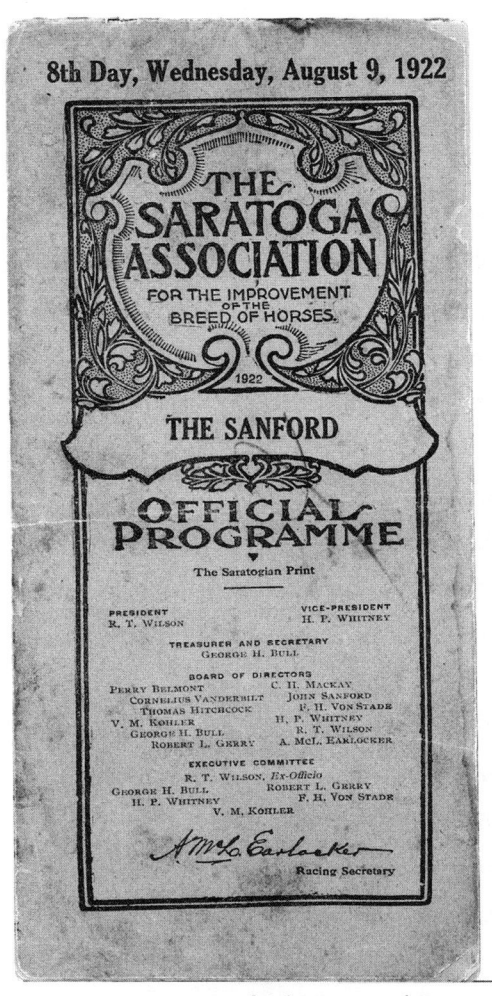

The track program on Sanford Memorial Day, 1922.

by top quality racing. The tradition of Saratoga as a summit meeting of leading stables traces to its beginning in the mid-19th century. Francis Morris, August Belmont, Stephen Sanford, E. J. "Lucky" Baldwin, the Lorillards, James R. Keene, and the Dwyer Brothers were among the powerful outfits that came to Saratoga.

Top stables continued their annual visits to Saratoga in the 20th century, as historic races such as the Travers, Alabama, Saratoga Cup, Flash, and Spinaway grew in stature. Several left a lasting imprint on Saratoga history during a period of prosperity.

The Whitneys

Other than the initial organized meeting in 1863, perhaps no other single event in Saratoga racing history was as important as the purchase of the track by a syndicate led by William C. Whitney in 1900.

In a brief career on the turf, he bred four champions, twice led the list of American owners in terms of earnings, and revitalized the oldest race course in the United States.

Following his death in 1904, the bloodstock from his estate was auctioned by Fasig-Tipton Company at Madison Square Garden. For more than a century, and continuing to the present day, the blood of Whitney breeding has continued to produce high quality thoroughbreds. His son Harry Payne Whitney was the leading buyer at the sale, and he bred numerous champions that won major races at Saratoga.

The aforementioned Regret, along with Equipoise and Top Flight, all became members of the racing Hall of Fame in Saratoga Springs. Although he raced once as a two-year-old at Saratoga, finishing second in the Saratoga Special of 1930 to Jamestown, Equipoise made his mark as an older horse at the Spa. He won the Wilson and Whitney as a four-year-old in 1932, and returned the following season to repeat in the Wilson and capture the prestigious Saratoga Cup at a mile and three-quarters.

Top Flight was a filly for the ages. As a two-year-old of 1931, she defeated males in the Saratoga Special and won the Spinaway over members of her own sex. She was unbeaten in seven starts as a juvenile, also defeating males in the Belmont Futurity and Pimlico Futurity. Top Flight was never beaten by a filly in 12 races, and won the Alabama Stakes at Saratoga as a three-year-old.

Harry Payne Whitney died in 1930, and Equipoise and Top Flight were campaigned by his son, Cornelius Vanderbilt Whitney. It is fitting that with such a family history, C.V. Whitney's racing and breeding would win many trophies at Saratoga. Four of them came in the race named for his father, which was inaugurated in 1928. He won the Whitney Handicap with Equipoise (1932), Counterpoint (1952), State Dinner (1980) and Silver Buck (1982). Counterpoint was the reigning Horse of the Year at the time, having won the Belmont Stakes and Jockey Club Gold Cup in 1951. He won the Travers with Fisherman (1954), Tompion (1960) and Chompion (1968).

In the mid-1950's, with his horses conditioned by Hall of Fame trainer Sylvester Veitch, C.V. Whitney registered an impressive run of victories. In particular, the 1954 season was marked by a terrific statistical accomplishment. Through the first fourteen days of the meet, Whitney runners won 16 of 32 starts, including the American Legion Handicap and Travers Stakes with Fisherman, the Saratoga Handicap with Cold Command, and the Test Stakes with Dispute. At the point of the Test Stakes, which came on day nine, the stable had won 12 of 20 starts.

Whitney also made a mark in Saratoga's two prestigious races for juveniles, the Spinaway and Hopeful. He won the former with Top Flight (1931) and Silver True (1966), and the latter with Red Rain (1935), Tompion (1959) and Banquet Table (1976). Another good juvenile at Saratoga was Career Boy, winner of the United States Hotel and Grand Union Stakes in 1955. Career Boy would go on to be champion grass horse in the United States, and was one of five champions bred by C.V. Whitney in addition to Handcuff, First Flight, Counterpoint, and Silver Spoon. In all, he bred 176 stakes winners, and among his major contributions to the breed was his purchase in 1940 of the stallion Mahmoud, winner of the 1936 Epsom Derby, from the Aga Khan.

He died in late 1992 at his Cady Hill home in Saratoga Springs, and his widow Marylou continued the family tradition. And as did Harry Payne decades earlier, she acquired mares with Whitney blood for her own stable. Although C.V. downplayed the idea of her as an active racing owner when she married him in 1958, she carried on with purpose. The author recalls a meeting with Marylou at the barn of Hall of Fame trainer T. J. Kelly one morning during the 1993 racing season at Saratoga. She arrived with notebooks of research on Whitney blood, and talked of nicking patterns that involved Mahmoud. Nicking refers to the matching of thoroughbred families that are often successful in producing stakes horses.

Marylou was thoroughly enjoying her racing experience. "I think anyone in the world who is retired and who has a little money – make that lots of money – should get involved in racing," she said. "Instead of going to the golf course, which you can do anyways, get out here in the morning and get a whole new lease on life."

Remarried to John Hendrickson, she bred the Eclipse Award

champion three-year-old filly of 2003 in Bird Town, winner of the Kentucky Oaks. Bird Town's younger half-brother Birdstone won the Travers Stakes in 2004 at Saratoga, where he had broken his maiden impressively at first asking the previous summer. Along with the Travers, Birdstone won a trio of the most important races in New York, winning the Champagne Stakes as a juvenile, and the Belmont Stakes prior to his Travers victory. Bird Town and Birdstone are out of the mare Dear Birdie, by Storm Bird. Dear Birdie's mother Hush Dear, grandmother You All, and great-grandmother Honey Dear are all Whitney mares.

Marylou Whitney was honored with the Eclipse Award of Merit in 2011, the same award received by C. V. Whitney in 1985 following his retirement from the turf.

Greentree Stable

Decade after decade, Mrs. Payne Whitney's thoroughbreds of the Greentree Stable compiled an awesome record at Saratoga.

Her champions Untidy, Twenty Grand and Devil Diver all won major stakes at Saratoga. Untidy won the Alabama Stakes in 1923, while Twenty Grand won the Travers and Saratoga Cup on the way to Horse of the Year honors in 1931. A second Travers winner was Shut Out in 1942. Devil Diver, in 1941, broke his maiden and won the Sanford and Hopeful stakes. During the Saratoga-at-Belmont meets of World War II, he won the Whitney and Wilson downstate in 1944. The stable won a second Hopeful with Outing Class in 1962.

The trio of champions is just the beginning. Greentree runners captured eight editions of the Sanford Stakes, a group that in addition to Devil Diver also included Tom Fool (1951) and Fuzzbuster (1978). Six trophies from the prestigious Whitney went to Greentree, with St. Brideaux (1931), Swing and Sway (1942), One Hitter (1951), Tom Fool (1953), and Cohoes (1958) joining Devil Diver on the list.

The historic Spinaway Stakes, the oldest stakes for two-year-old fillies in the United States, went to Greentree runners Goose Egg (1929), Easy Day (1932), Sunday Evening (1949), and Register (1955). Greentree won the Saranac four times, with Cherry Pie (1923), Cohoes (1957), Stage Door Johnny (1968) and Buckaroo (1978).

Other major stakes won by Greentree include two editions of the Test and Saratoga Special, plus the Diana and Adirondack.

The Wideners

Joseph E. Widener, his nephew George D. Widener and his wife

Mrs. George D. Widener captured major trophies at Saratoga Race Course during much of the 20th century. The Shillelah Steeplechase was won by Joseph E. on opening day in 1915 with El Bart. Fifty-five years later, George D. won the Schuylerville Stakes with Patelin in 1970. In between, there was scarcely a season that a Widener did not make racing news at Saratoga.

Joseph E. Widener enjoyed a terrific season at the Spa in 1926, winning the Flash with Osmand, the Test with Ruthenia, the Saratoga Special with Chance Shot, the Grand Union Hotel with Kiev, and the North American Steeplechase with Lorenzo, winner also of the Saratoga Steeplechase in 1927. Osmand would win the Saranac in 1927, while the very good runner Chance Shot won the Saratoga Handicap and Merchants' and Citizens' Stakes in 1928. Widener also won the Grand Union Hotel with Haste in 1925, and again in 1934 with Chance Sun. He won a second Test Stakes with Buckup in 1931 and another edition of the Merchants' and Citizens' with Curate in 1931.

Joseph E. Widener was also an advocate of pari-mutuel wagering as a way for both tracks and states to have a secure economic future. He proposed it as early as 1932, noting that it was in use in Australia.[5]

George D. Widener won five editions of the Travers Stakes, the signature event of Saratoga racing, symbolic of his love of tradition and historic New York races. It is the oldest stakes race for three-year-olds in the United States.

Several of his champions won major events at the Spa. Jamestown won the Flash Stakes in 1930, a race won by Widener nine times. Jamestown also captured the Grand Union Hotel, Saratoga Special and United States Hotel stakes that summer. The Saratoga Special he won four times, with St. James (1923), Battlefield (1950) and Pontifex (1969) in addition to Jamestown.

Widener won the Sanford Stakes five times, with Parasol (1923), Hi-Jack (1929), Birch Rod (1938), Cornish Prince (1964) and Yorkville (1966). He won the rich Hopeful Stakes four times, with Jack High (1928), Battlefield (1950), Jaipur (1961) and Bold Hour (1966).

It was Jaipur who won one of thoroughbred racing's most thrilling contests in the 1962 Travers Stakes. He and Ridan battled every step of the ten furlongs required in the "Midsummer Derby." With Ridan on the inside and Jaipur alongside, the pair raced together all the way, and Jaipur emerged the narrowest of winners at the end of a mile and a quarter in 2:01 3/5, the fastest time in the race since Man o' War in 1920. Widener's other victories in the Travers came with Eight Thirty (1939), Lights Up (1950), Battlefield (1951) and Crewman (1963).

Eight Thirty won four major stakes for George D. Widener during the 1939 season. He captured the Saratoga Handicap, Wilson Mile, Travers and Whitney.

The filly counterpart to the Travers is the hallowed Alabama Stakes, and Widener won it with Stefanita in 1943 and What A Treat in 1965. Both were champion three-year-old fillies. Stefanita's victory came at Belmont Park, as Saratoga racing was conducted downstate during 1943-45 due to World War II travel restrictions.

In addition to the aforementioned Jamestown, George D. Widener won the Flash Stakes with Felix (1924), Jack High (1928), Eight Thirty (1938), Overdrawn (1940), Plebiscite (1944), Jaipur (1961), Bold Hour (1966) and Pontifex (1969).

Mrs. George D. Widener bred and raced Evening Out, the champion two-year-old filly of 1953, who won the Schuylerville and Spinaway stakes that year in dominant fashion. She also bred and raced Belle de Nuit, winner of the Test Stakes in 1966.

Alfred G. Vanderbilt

When Dehere won the Saratoga Special, Sanford and Hopeful Stakes at the 1993 Saratoga meeting, it attracted much attention as a rare occurrence within the time frame of one month, from July 29 to August 29. Somewhat forgotten in Saratoga juvenile history was the four-race sweep of Alfred G. Vanderbilt's immortal Native Dancer in 1952. From August 4 to August 30, he won the Flash, Saratoga Special, Grand Union Hotel and Hopeful to remain unbeaten in his first six career starts to that point. Bred and raced by Vanderbilt, he was a son of Polynesian out of Geisha. Vanderbilt's champion Discovery, the sire of Geisha, compiled a tremendous Saratoga record.

One can only wonder about Native Dancer's place in history had he not lost the Kentucky Derby in 1953. It was his only defeat in 22 starts, in a career marked by 18 major stakes victories that also included the remaining two-thirds of the Triple Crown, the Preakness and Belmont. At Saratoga he won the Travers Stakes in addition to the juvenile quartet, and concluded his career as a four-year-old in 1954 by winning the Oneonta Handicap.

The great gray also made a direct and everlasting contribution to the breed during his short stud career, having died at age 17 in 1967. Native Dancer sired the brilliant Raise A Native, the sire of Alydar, Exclusive Native and Mr. Prospector. He also sired the filly Natalma, who finished first in the 1959 Spinaway Stakes at Saratoga, but was disqualified to third. She would later produce the immortal sire and champion runner Northern Dancer.

Discovery, at Saratoga, was something else. He won three consecutive editions of the 10-furlong Whitney Handicap during

THE SARATOGA ASSOCIATION
FOR THE IMPROVEMENT OF THE BREED OF HORSES
6 AND 8 EAST 46TH STREET
NEW YORK

Discovery won the Whitney at Saratoga in 1934, 1935 and 1936.

1934-36 by a total of 22 lengths. In 1934, he won the historic Kenner Stakes prior to his Whitney score. In 1935, he won the Wilson by six lengths in "eased up" fashion and the Merchants' and Citizens' by two, the latter under 139 pounds. Discovery carried 126 pounds in his second Whitney victory, conceding 26 pounds to second-place Esposa.

Discovery's campaign of 1936 at Saratoga consisted of five starts within a span of 28 days. He kicked things off on August 1 with a victory in the Saratoga Handicap under 132 pounds at 10 furlongs, spotting 23 pounds to second-place Mantagna. He returned on August 5 to win the Wilson by eight lengths. Discovery next started in the Merchants' and Citizens' on August 8 under 143 pounds. He tired to finish fifth and last, beaten 6 ½ lengths by Esposa, who carried 100 pounds. Off for 13 days, he captured his third Whitney on August 22 under 126 pounds by ten lengths while giving old rival Esposa five pounds. Discovery completed this Saratoga summer by finishing second to Granville in the Saratoga Cup at a mile and three quarters in the slop, giving his three-year-old rival ten pounds. They were the only two in the race.

Both were champions in the first formal voting conducted by Daily Racing Form, with Granville the Horse of the Year and Discovery the handicap champion.

Other major stakes captured by Vanderbilt at Saratoga include the Spinaway with Now What in 1939 and Good Move in 1960, and the Sanford in 1940 with Good Turn. He had an outstanding season in 1935, winning the Test and Saranac with Good Gamble; the United States Hotel with Postage Due; and the Schuylerville with Parade Girl. His good runner Cousin won the Saratoga Special and Hopeful in 1951.

Brookmeade Stable

Horses bred or raced by Isabel Dodge Sloane's Brookmeade Stable won stakes races at Saratoga from the 1920's to the 1970's. Her great champion Sword Dancer won the Travers Stakes in 1959, a year in which he earned honors as Horse of the Year, champion three-year-old, and champion handicap horse. Sword Dancer was the second of her two Travers winners, the other being Inlander in 1933.

Brookmeade Stable won virtually every major event at Saratoga, including several that have passed into history such as the Shillelah Steeplechase, Huron, Delaware, and Saratoga handicaps. At the time of this writing, there are six renowned juvenile stakes at Saratoga, three for females and three for males, and Brookmeade Stable won them all. Victories in the Adirondack Stakes came with Riant (1953), in the Schuylerville Stakes with Teacher (1939) and Atalanta (1950, and in the Spinaway Stakes with Atalanta (1950) and Gandharva (1954). Brookmeade won the Sanford with Psychic Bid (1934) and Inseparable (1947), the Saratoga Special with Grand Admiral (1946) and More Sun (1949), and the Hopeful Stakes with Brooms (1927) and Psychic Bid (1934).

One of the nation's prizes for older males is the Whitney, and Brookmeade captured it with Caesar's Ghost (1933) and First Aid (1955). The Alabama was won by Handcuff (1938), while the Test was won at Belmont Park in 1945 with Safeguard. Brookmeade Stable won the Diana Handicap three times, with Pomayya (1942), Bonnet Ann (1943 at Belmont), and Ouija (1950). There were also three wins in the Saranac, with Sunglow (1950), Bold (1951) and First Aid (1953).

Wheatley Stable

In decade after decade as the 20th century unfolded, the Wheatley Stable of Mrs. Henry Carnegie Phipps won the major trophies of Saratoga racing. Nixie won the Test and Alabama in 1928, while Hard Tack won the Saranac in 1929. Two more Test Stakes were won by Bold Consort in 1963 and Discipline in 1965, while a second Alabama was won by High Bid in 1959. Wheatley

Stable also won two more editions of the Saranac, with Full Flight in 1954 and Nasco in 1958.

Slapdash won the first of four editions of the Schuylerville in 1933, followed by Irish Jay (1959), Bold Princess (1962), and Bright Sun (1969). Wheatley Stable also took down the Adirondack with Matterhorn in 1938, and the Spinaway with Merry Lassie in 1937 and Irish Jay in 1959. Wheatley Stable also won two of the the three surviving major stakes for males, beginning with Bold Lad's victory in the Hopeful in 1964, a race they also won with What A Pleasure in 1967 and Irish Castle in 1969. King Emperor won the Sanford in 1968. Wheatley's champion filly and great broodmare Misty Morn won the Diana Handicap in 1955. The stable captured the Whitney Handicap in 1967 with Stupendous.

Ogden Phipps, the son of Mrs. Henry Carnegie Phipps, and his son Ogden Mills "Dinny" Phipps continued the tradition of breeding and racing champions at Saratoga throughout the 20th century and into the 21st century. Ogden Phipps's Buckpasser won the Hopeful in 1965 and Travers in 1966. In 1988 his immortal unbeaten filly Personal Ensign won the Whitney Handicap, and his Easy Goer won the Whitney and Travers in 1989. In 2004, Storm Flag Flying won the Personal Ensign Handicap. Rhythm, bred and raced by Ogden Mills "Dinny" Phipps, won the Travers in 1990.

Colonel E.R. Bradley

Known for his love of the Kentucky Derby and for naming his horses with the letter B, Colonel Edward Riley Bradley was a prominent figure at Saratoga during the 1920's and 1930's. His four Kentucky Derby victories, with Behave Yourself (1921), Bubbling Over (1926), Burgoo King (1932), and Brokers Tip (1933), were the most by an owner until Calumet Farm captured eight.

Perhaps his most talented runner was Bimelech, the champion two-year-old of 1939 and again champion of his division in 1940. Bimelech won his first eight races, including the Saratoga Special and Hopeful Stakes in 1939. The eighth was the Derby Trial in 1940, raising Bradley's hopes he would get a fifth Kentucky Derby, but Bimelech weakened late in the stretch to finish second. At Saratoga that summer, a broken bone sent Bimelech to the sidelines, and an emotional Bradley called him the best horse he had ever owned.[6]

Such a claim covered lots of ground, for Bradley also campaigned champion Blue Larkspur, who won the Saratoga Special in 1928. Bradley won a third Special with Boxthorn in 1934. The Adirondack he won with Blockhead (1925), Bird Flower (1934) and Beanie M. (1935). Bradley won the prestigious Spinaway with Blue Warbler in 1924. In addition to Bimelech's score in the Hopeful, he also won with the filly Bazaar in 1933 and Blue Border in 1946. Bazaar returned the following summer to win the Test Stakes. His filly Befuddle won the Schuylerville in 1923.

Bradley won the Alabama Stakes with Barn Swallow in 1933, and the Saranac with Bless Me in 1942. He also won several stakes that are no longer on the Saratoga calendar, such as the United States Hotel in 1934 with Balladier and the Grand Union Hotel with By Jiminy in 1943 at Belmont Park. Bradley runners also won stakes such as the Glens Falls, North Creek, Burnt Hills, Amsterdam, and Albany during this period. His steeplechase performer Barometer was one of the best in 1932, winning the Beverwyck, North American and Saratoga steeplechases at the Spa.

The death of August Belmont II

On December 10, 1924, August Belmont II died suddenly at age 71 in New York City. A chairman of The Jockey Club, he was the son of August Belmont, who was a supporter of thoroughbred racing in the post-Civil War era in the north. The younger Belmont continued to operate his father's Nursery Stud near Lexington, Kentucky, and he bred many outstanding runners who won major stakes races at Saratoga.

Foremost was the immortal Man o' War. There was also Beldame,

THE SARATOGA ASSOCIATION
FOR THE IMPROVEMENT OF THE BREED OF HORSES
6 AND 8 EAST 46TH STREET
NEW YORK

Clare Court, a private training track built by August Belmont II during the "Whitney Revival."

winner of the Alabama Stakes and Saratoga Cup in 1904, two trophies on the way to honors as America's best horse and champion three-year-old filly. Belmont also bred champions Rock View, winner of the Travers in 1913; Friar Rock, winner of the Saratoga Cup in 1916; Hourless, winner of the Grand Union Hotel in 1916; and Chance Play, winner of the Saratoga Cup in 1927. Other stakes winners at Saratoga bred by Belmont include Masterman, winner of the United States Hotel in 1901; Lord of the Vale, winner of the Saratoga Handicap in 1904; Fair Play, winner of the Flash in 1907; Field Mouse, winner of the Delaware and Saranac handicaps in 1909; Stromboli, winner of the Saranac in 1914; Malachite winner of the Alabama in 1916; and Chance Shot, winner of the Saratoga Special in 1926 and Saratoga Handicap in 1928.

Belmont also built a private training track at Saratoga that is today known as Clare Court. Access to Clare Court is a tunnel that runs under the track itself, then connects to the barn area within the half-mile oval.

In early 1925, Joseph E. Widener purchased much of the bloodstock of the estate of Belmont, which consisted of the stallions Fair Play, Messenger and Hourless, and 65 broodmares for a reported $500,000.[7] Widener announced he would sell the acquisitions at Nursery Stud on May 15, the day before the Kentucky Derby.

Leading turf men and women from major centers in the United States and Canada attended the sale, which netted $783,000, and at which Widener retained Fair Play at $100,000.

Saratoga's Tommy Luther

Jockey Tommy Luther, a native of Millington, Illinois, came to Saratoga Race Course for the first time in 1928, under contract to the Coldstream Stable. Luther would eventually make Saratoga Springs his home, and died at Saratoga Hospital on January 27, 2001 at age 92. He played an important role in the foundation of the Jockeys' Guild, motivated by his concern for a fellow jockey killed in a racing accident in 1927. One of his biggest victories came aboard Crystal Pennant in the rich Coffroth Handicap at Tijuana in 1928. He was honored by the Jockeys' Guild in 1991 with a Founders Pin, and in 1999 at Saratoga Race Course on opening day with a race named in his honor.

Trainers Rowe and Fitzsimmons

The 1929 season at Saratoga was marked by great racing, immense crowds, the loss of a great trainer in James Rowe, and the accomplishments of another great trainer, the legendary "Sunny Jim" Fitzsimmons.

Rowe died at Saratoga Hospital during the 1929 racing season at the Spa. He had ridden at Saratoga in 1872, winning the Saratoga Cup that year aboard Harry Bassett. Rowe's list of Hall of Fame champions is staggering. He trained Hindoo, Colin, Miss Woodford, Commando, Peter Pan, Sysonby, Luke Blackburn, Maskette, Whisk Broom II and Regret. He was elected to the Hall of Fame in its inaugural class of 1955, along with trainers A. Jack Joyner, Samuel C. Hildreth, Thomas J. Healey, John W. Rogers, and W. P. Burch.

The two-year-olds of 1929 were quite a bunch, with Gallant Fox, Whichone, and Boojum all winning juvenile stakes. Boojum and Whichone finished 1-2 in the Hopeful Stakes for H. P. Whitney. Whitney also captured the Travers Stakes with Beacon Hill in 1929. Crowds were estimated at 40,000 for both the Travers and Hopeful that summer.

Fitzsimmons grabbed Saratoga by the throat on opening day, July 29. He won the Flash Stakes with Gallant Fox for Belair Stud, and the Saratoga Handicap with Diavolo for the Wheatley Stable. Two days later he won the Schuylerville Stakes with Flying Gal for Belair. On August 7 it was the Saranac with Hard Tack, and on August 9 the Albany Handicap with Peto. On August 31, Diavolo won the Saratoga Cup, a race that Fitzsimmons would win ten times. "Sunny Jim" had been making a mark at the Spa for many years prior, and would continue to be a dominant force for decades.

Gallant Fox would win the Triple Crown in 1930, and get another Saratoga Cup that summer for Fitzsimmons. He did not win the Travers, losing to 100-to-1 shot Jim Dandy in one of racing's most famous upsets. During the 1929 meeting, Jim Dandy had won the Grand Union Hotel Stakes at long odds; both his upsets were on muddy tracks. Fitzsimmons won his second Triple Crown with Omaha in 1935. In 1936, he won yet another Saratoga Cup with Granville, winner also of the Travers that year.

"Sunny Jim" was still going strong in the 1950's, training a pair of greats in Nashua and Bold Ruler. The former won the Grand Union Hotel and Hopeful in 1954. Both won Horse of the Year honors, joining Granville in that regard. Fitzsimmons won the Alabama Stakes eight times during his career, and was elected to the Hall of Fame in 1958.

The death of Richard T. Wilson

At the end of 1929, Saratoga Association president Richard T. Wilson died in New York City on December 29. A banker and major supporter of the turf, he was credited as one of the prime movers in William C. Whitney's purchase of the track in 1900.[8] Wilson oversaw many improvements to the track facilities. He was also an innovator, creating the Lady Owners Handicap at the 1929 meeting. It was won by Greentree Stable's Goose Egg, and Wilson presented the trophy to Mrs. Payne Whitney. Wilson also created and hosted a popular dinner for subscribers to the Saratoga Special Stakes, held at The Brook Club in Saratoga Springs. He bred and owned Campfire, the champion two-year-old of 1916 when he won the Sanford, Saratoga Special and Hopeful Stakes. Campfire won six of nine starts that year for earnings of $49,735, tops among all horses in the United States that season.

In honor of Wilson, the Wilson Mile was inaugurated in 1930. It started out of a chute, parallel to Nelson Avenue, and joined the main track at the seven-eighths pole on the clubhouse turn. After having been run also at Belmont Park and Jamaica, it was discontinued after the 1958 edition. Famous winners of the event include Hall of Fame members Equipoise, Discovery and Gallorette. The chute itself was dismantled after the 1970 season and the land used for additional clubhouse parking. In a short-lived revival, the New York Racing Association brought back one-mile races by building a new chute at the same location in 1992, although at more of an angle upon entering the main track than the original.

Equine Stars of the 1930's

As the 1930's got underway, there was much anticipation of

seeing Gallant Fox return to the Spa. He had become the second winner of the Triple Crown earlier in the season, and his expected appearance in the Travers Stakes received lots of coverage in the media. He was unbeaten in six starts as a three-year-old as the Saratoga season got underway, having also won the Wood Memorial, Dwyer and Arlington Classic in addition to the Kentucky Derby, Preakness and Belmont. During the buildup to the Travers, Gallant Fox's main foe was considered to be Whichone, who had already swept through the Saranac, Whitney and Miller at the 1930 meeting. He won the Whitney on just two days rest after the Saranac. But once again Jim Dandy, as he had in 1929 in the Grand Union Hotel, struck on a muddy Saratoga track on Travers Day and shocked Gallant Fox.

When C. V. Whitney's two-year-old filly Top Flight arrived at Saratoga in 1931, she was already a stakes winner, having captured the Clover Stakes at Aqueduct in her career debut on June 17 and the Lassie Stakes at Arlington Park on July 8, both against members of her own sex. She moved outside that group to win the Saratoga Special on August 15 in her next start, and followed with the historic Spinaway on August 22. When racing returned downstate, she won the Matron and Futurity at Belmont, the latter over males on September 19. The Hall of Fame filly completed her juvenile season by winning the Pimlico Futurity on November 7. Finishing third was

Burgoo King, who would go on to win the 1932 Kentucky Derby. She earned $219,000 as a two-year-old, tops among all racehorses in the nation that year. Top Flight returned to Saratoga as a three-year-old to win the Alabama Stakes.

On the same day that Top Flight won the Spinaway, Greentree Stable's Twenty Grand captured the Travers Stakes. Yet another champion of this period to grace the Spa, he captured the Saratoga Cup on closing day, September 5, winning by 10 lengths at one and three-quarter miles for a prestigious double. Twenty Grand also won the Wood Memorial, Kentucky Derby, Belmont Stakes, Lawrence Realization, and Jockey Club Gold Cup in 1931. Thus, that summer at Saratoga saw the champion two-year-old filly in Top Flight, and America's best horse and champion three-year-old male in Twenty Grand.

During this period of the Great Depression, C.V. Whitney's Equipoise made an unforgettable impression on Saratoga fans. His appearance was especially welcome as a boost to gate revenue, which was the main source of income for the Saratoga Association at this time. On August 6, 1932, he won the Wilson at one mile, and one week later the Whitney at a mile and a quarter, both with authority. Equipoise returned to win a second Wilson on August 3, 1933. At the same meet, on September 2, he won the Saratoga Cup at a mile and three-quarters in impressive fashion. Both Equipoise and Alfred G. Vanderbilt's Discovery were hugely popular stars at Saratoga in the 1930's, helping the Saratoga Association's earnings.

A unique example of sportsmanship occurred at the 1935 Saratoga meeting in the Saratoga Special on August 10. C.V. Whitney's Red Rain and Elmer Dale Shaffer's Coldstream finished on even terms. Whitney and Shaffer, in front of stands packed with an estimated 25,000 fans, flipped a coin to determine the winner, which landed in favor of Shaffer and Coldstream. Saratoga Association president George Bull asked about the coin flip and when told about it, decided to award a trophy to both, bringing cheers from thousands.[9]

The 1936 season opened on July 29, and Maemare Farm's Maedic won the Flash Stakes. The 28-day meeting concluded on August 29, when Maedic won the Hopeful Stakes. In between, he also captured the Saratoga Sales, Sanford and Grand Union Hotel to win five juvenile stakes at the Spa. Despite this summer accomplishment, he would not be division champion, that honor going to Pompoon, who won the Futurity at Belmont. Maedic was trained by George Phillips, who was suspended indefinitely during the 1936 meeting for a positive saliva test on another Maemare farm horse, Maerial. The substance was coramine. Phillips was later reinstated, as was the groom, by the New York State Racing Commission.

The star two-year-old of 1939 was E. R. Bradley's Bimelech, the division champion and winner of the Saratoga Special and Hopeful at the Spa. The star three-year-old was George D. Widener's Eight Thirty, who ran the table in four starts in a manner similar to the aforementioned War Admiral. On August 2, Eight Thirty won the Wilson Mile, rested for two days, and won the Saratoga Handicap at a mile and one-quarter on August 5. On August 15, trainer Bert Mulholland worked Eight Thirty a mile and a quarter in a terrific 2:04 in preparation for the Travers four days later. Eight Thirty won the Travers on August 19, and four days later won another race at a mile and a quarter, the Whitney Handicap. Such a program of racing for a fit horse was not unusual in this era, although in contemporary times it is nonexistent.

Saratoga rejects the famous match between War Admiral and Seabiscuit

The reigning Horse of the Year in 1938, based on his sweep of the Triple Crown and unbeaten season in 1937, was War Admiral. And the reigning handicap champion the same year was five-year-old Seabsicuit, a year older than War Admiral and the winner of such races in 1937 as the San Juan Capistrano, Brooklyn, and Massachusetts handicaps in a transcontinental campaign. Both horses were nominated to stakes at Saratoga in 1938, and the idea of a match race at the Spa was on plenty of minds. Saratoga Association president George Bull opposed the idea, saying he was against match racing and would not put much pressure on the respective owners for one at Saratoga.

"Saratoga wants no part of that kind of thing," he said. "Saratoga is run only for the improvement of the breed of horses. It is one of the few tracks in the world where that circumstance exists."[10] The excitement over such a race at Saratoga was heightened by the reservation of stalls at Saratoga by Charles S. Howard, owner of Seabiscuit, in the Alfred G. Vanderbilt barn. But only War Admiral raced at Saratoga in 1938, winning the Wilson, Saratoga Handicap, Whitney, and Saratoga Cup within a one-month span. Seabiscuit did not race at Saratoga in 1938, although he had done so in 1935 and 1936. The match race, however, came about later that year when Vanderbilt, a majority owner of Pimlico Race Course, invited the pair to run in the second edition of the Pimlico Special on November 1. Seabiscuit was the winner by four lengths.

War Admiral was one of several top Glen Riddle runners to win stakes in this era. In addition to War Admiral, the stable won another Saratoga Cup in 1932 with War Hero, who also won the Travers Stakes that year. Another stakes winner in 1932 was Speed Boat, winner of the Adirondack who returned to win the Test Stakes in 1933. War Glory, in 1933, won the Saranac for Glen Riddle. The outfit also won two editions of the Alabama Stakes, with Maid at Arms in 1925 and War Hazard in 1941.

Chapter IV
PARI-MUTUELS ARRIVE AND WORLD WAR II 1940-1945

CONCERN OVER STATISTICS AND THE FUTURE

The era of book-making at the New York tracks was over, and the new pari-mutuel machines were first used in a rehearsal at downstate Jamaica on April 12, 1940. On opening day, July 29, 1940, pari-mutuel wagering came to Saratoga Race Course. And with it came the beginning of statistical comparisons with downstate tracks, in terms of attendance and betting, that would threaten the quality of summer racing in Saratoga Springs. The Saratoga Association had 307 mutuel windows open, with the track and state each getting five percent of the betting dollar.

Daily average betting at the downstate tracks was approximately $600,000, so there was interest in how tradition-bound Saratoga would do in comparison. The opening day crowd of 7,701 wagered $262,526, a disappointment by any measure. There were some problems with the new machines, and Monday was usually one of the slower days of the week at the Spa, so observers figured things would improve as the 30-day meet continued. However, the

THE SARATOGA ASSOCIATION
FOR THE IMPROVEMENT OF THE BREED OF HORSES
6 AND 8 EAST 46TH STREET
NEW YORK

Diagram of the betting rings, where bookmakers took bets before pari-mutuel betting came to Saratoga in 1940.

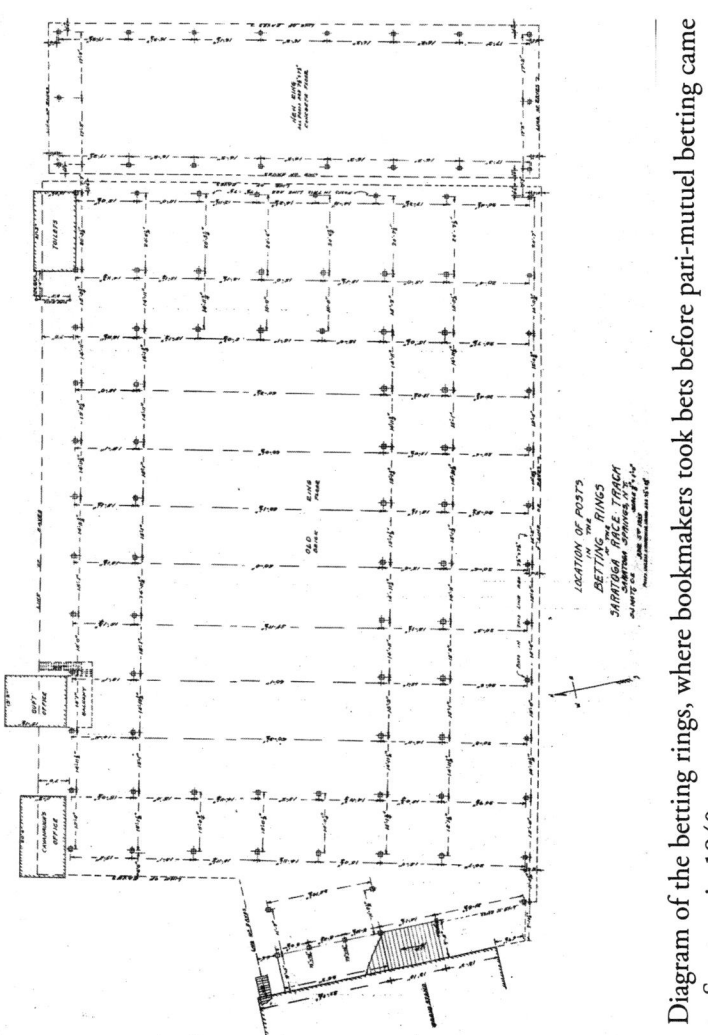

numbers dropped on Tuesday, with 4,780 wagering $183,714, but by Saturday, August 3, handle hit $574,989 with 15,500 fans in attendance.

The following Saturday saw betting hit $637,529, with 17,904 fans watching a two-year-old named Whirlaway win the Saratoga Special. The great Calumet runner that day began a series of stakes victories at Saratoga that helped establish a mark unique to this day. In 1941 he won the Travers Stakes, thus becoming the only horse in history to have won the Triple Crown and the Midsummer Derby.

Betting hit $774,393 on Travers Day, Saturday August 17. A crowd of 20,664 watched Belair Stud's Fenelon win the event, with the trophy being presented by James J. Wadsworth, the great grandson of William R. Travers. The 1940 season ended on August 31, with 11,939 fans betting $353,053 and watching Whirlaway win the Hopeful Stakes. Attendance for the first year of pari-mutuel wagering came in at 282,200, an increase over the 1939 figure of 256,770.

Attendance continued upward in 1941, hitting 318,816, but remained virtually static in 1942 at 316,785. With a touch of humor, the Saratoga Association on the closing day of August 30, 1941, carded a race called "The Hopeless," for maiden 3-year-olds, which was on the same card as the famous Hopeful Stakes.

Transportation restrictions and gas rationing, due to World War II, were beginning to hurt Saratoga, with attendance at less than 4,000 on two occasions during the 30-day stand of 1942. The practice of New York tracks contributing to the war effort was underway, with Saratoga hosting "Russian War Relief Day" on July 28. Saturday still delivered, though, with the last four each topping 13,000 in attendance. As the war years proceeded, the Saratoga Association continued to donate receipts to various organizations involved in the effort, including Saratoga Hospital.

A noteworthy accomplishment in the final year before racing moved to Belmont involved W. E. Boeing's juvenile male Devil's Thumb. He became the second youngster to capture five stakes races at Saratoga. After finishing second in the Flash Stakes on July 27, he won the United States Hotel on August 1, the Saratoga Sales Stakes on August 5, the Sanford on August 12, the Grand Union Hotel on August 22, and the Hopeful on August 29.

Thomas and Anne Clare

The Saratoga track superintendent at this time was Mrs. Anne Clare, who succeeded her husband Tom Clare upon his death in 1940. The only woman to have such a job at a major American track at the time, she had been his assistant for the previous 16 years.

THE SARATOGA ASSOCIATION
FOR THE IMPROVEMENT OF THE BREED OF HORSES
6 AND 8 EAST 46TH STREET
NEW YORK

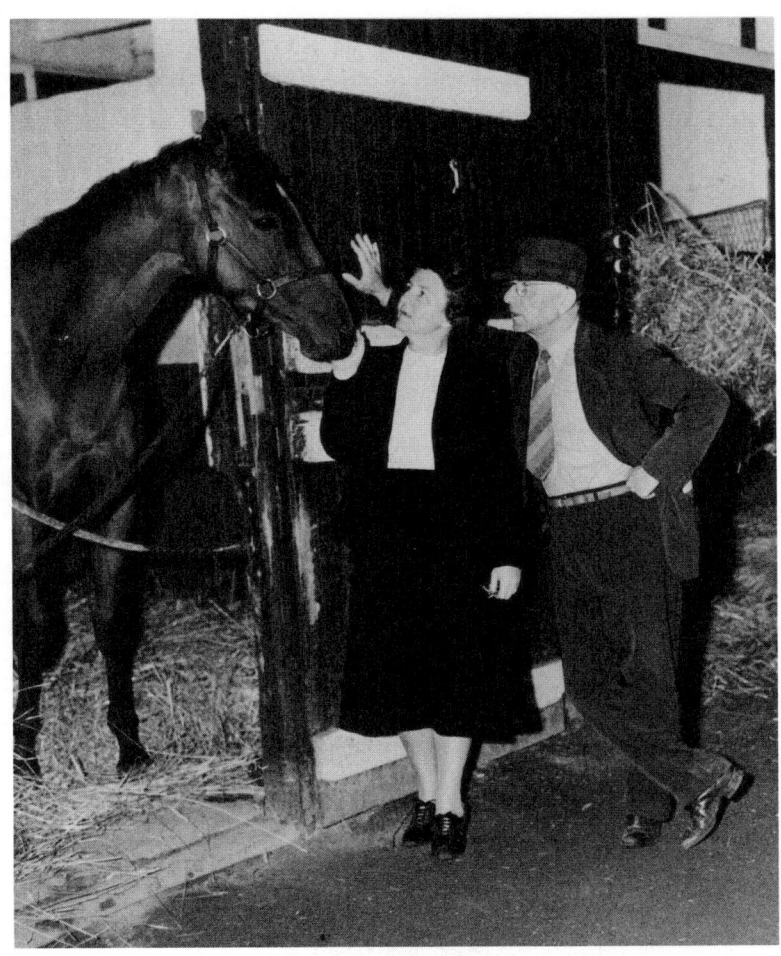

Thomas and Anne Clare, both track superintendents at Saratoga.

THE SARATOGA ASSOCIATION
FOR THE IMPROVEMENT OF THE BREED OF HORSES
6 AND 8 EAST 46TH STREET
NEW YORK

Mrs. Clare, born on the lower East Side of New York, supervised a crew of some 150, charged with maintaining grounds that included stables with 1,800 stalls, the main track, Horse Haven, Oklahoma Training Track, and Clare Court. The last-named is in honor of the family, and was built by August Belmont II.

Additionally, her supervisory duties included the Reading Room, the turf courses of the main and training track, and the steeplechase courses. The home of the Saratoga track superintendent, across the street from the main track on Union Avenue in Saratoga Springs, was built in 1934 for Mr. and Mrs. Clare. They were popular and respected figures on the American racing scene, from coast to coast.

Anne married into a family with decades of experience in the field. Tom received his Saratoga appointment from the Saratoga Association on January 17, 1924. His grandfather, William Clare, was the track superintendent of Jerome Park in Westchester, which was home to the American Jockey Club and had been built by Leonard Jerome in 1866. Jerome was one of the founders of Saratoga Race Course.

Mrs. Clare served as track superintendent from 1940 to 1960. She died in 1976.

"They loved their job and they loved the people in racing with whom they were associated," said Diana Burke, in an interview with the author on January 9, 2012. "It was such a different time for racing at Saratoga. It really was family, and the patrons who came here every summer really cared for the traditions of Saratoga racing." Burke is a niece, by marriage, of Anne Clare.

Saratoga at Belmont Park

The Saratoga races during 1943, 1944, and 1945 were conducted at Belmont Park. There was, however, a day of exhibition racing at the Oklahoma Training Track on July 4, 1943. With the support of the Saratoga Association and Greentree Stable, among others, several hundred fans watched races of a quarter-mile. This transfer of dates to Belmont stands as a dividing line in Saratoga racing history. Attendance at the 30 days of Belmont in 1943 was 539,396, compared to the 234,530 at Saratoga in 1942. In 1944 the figure soared to 690,730. The 1945 season consisted of 24 days, and the total attendance of 746,793 was phenomenal in view of six fewer days of racing than in 1944.

A letter to the Sports Editor of the *New York Times* published on August 14, 1943, reflected the views of downstate fans. The writer, who signed his name as D. Leonard on August 9, noted larger tax revenues to the state with racing at Belmont, as opposed to Saratoga, and said the downstate racing public wanted summer racing in the metropolitan area. The Saratoga Association surely did not miss the significance of business at Belmont. Three of the most profitable meetings in its long history came when racing was not conducted at Saratoga Race Course.

Greentree Stable's Devil Diver and Walter M. Jeffords's Pavot were two of the most accomplished runners during this period. The former, a foal of 1939, is a member of the Hall of Fame. At Saratoga, he won the Sanford and Hopeful in 1941. In 1944, he captured the Whitney and Wilson during the Spa session at Belmont. Pavot, a foal of 1942, won the United States Hotel, Saratoga Special, Grand Union Hotel, and Hopeful during a 28-day run at Belmont in 1944. In 1945, he was fourth and second, respectively, in the Travers and Whitney.

Pavot was one of several champions and major stakes winners of the Jeffords family to win trophies at Saratoga. They won four editions of the Travers Stakes, with Mars (1926), Natchez (1946), One Count (1952) and Piano Jim (1958). They won two more editions of the Saratoga Special in addition to Pavot's, with Golden Broom (1919) and Halberd (1942). Jeffords Stable runners won the Alabama Stakes with Regal Lily (1937) and Adile (1949), and the Whitney Handicap with Bateau (1929) and Trymenow (1945).

The stable also won stakes such as the Schuylerville, Diana,

Adirondack, Saranac, Hopeful, Saratoga Cup, and New York Turf Writers Cup Steeplechase.

Worries when racing returns to Saratoga

When racing returned to Saratoga in 1946, Pavot captured the Wilson Mile over the great mare Gallorette. And when it did return, the meeting was 24 days, or six shorter than in 1942. The Saratoga Association continued to run some of its dates downstate, the track being Jamaica in the post-war years. The idea and culture of the 24-day summer meeting in Saratoga Springs began to settle in the Spa city.

What *was* unsettling was the prospect of Saratoga losing its summer race meeting altogether, or seeing its exclusivity damaged by the powerful attendance and handle figures at Belmont Park during the war, and at Jamaica afterward. The author recalls the annual worries at the end of Saratoga meetings in the 1950's regarding the future of America's oldest thoroughbred track. The Greater New York Association, which owned and operated Aqueduct, Belmont, Jamaica and Saratoga, entertained the idea of continuous summer racing downstate. It was investing millions in a modernization of Aqueduct during 1955-59.

"Yes, there was some feeling on the board that maybe we should have continuous racing in [metropolitan] New York," said Alfred G. Vanderbilt to the author during the racing season of 1992 at Saratoga. "A lot of money had been spent at Aqueduct." Vanderbilt was a former board chairman of the New York Racing Association.

The Saratoga Springs community began to mobilize in 1956, with bi-partisan support for saving the traditional summer meet with exclusive racing days. Among those leading the effort were Addison Mallery, Mayor of Saratoga Springs; Arthur J. Kearney, president of the Saratoga Chamber of Commerce; Paul Hilleboe and William T. Ashton of the Chamber's racing committee; Joseph Hammer, Saratoga County Democratic chairman; and Fred G. Eaton, editor of the *Saratogian*.

"People here kept hearing threats of concurrent racing downstate," said Harry D. Snyder. "Along with the Chamber of Commerce initiative, people realized that political clout was also needed here."[1]

Snyder, along with fellow Democrat Bob Gass, and Republicans Michael Sweeney and John Nichols, the latter Saratoga County Republican chairman, worked as a four-person team to cover the political bases. State Assemblyman John Ostrander of Schuylerville, and State Senator Gilbert Steelye co-sponsored a bill to reserve 24 days of summer racing in Saratoga Springs, during which time there could be no racing downstate. Governor Averell Harriman signed the bill on April 23, 1957.

THE SARATOGA ASSOCIATION
FOR THE IMPROVEMENT OF THE BREED OF HORSES
6 AND 8 EAST 46TH STREET
NEW YORK

Chapter V
RETURN TO SARATOGA AND A NEW ORDER FOR THE FUTURE 1946-1955

RACING RETURNS TO SARATOGA SPRINGS

Following three World War II years at Belmont Park, racing returned to Saratoga Race Course on August 5, 1946, with a healthy crowd of 15,168 in attendance. It was a happy occasion for the citizens of Saratoga Springs, many of whom remembered the shut down of New York racing in 1911 and 1912 due to anti-gambling legislation. They also recalled no racing in 1896, the year when Saratoga fortunes hit bottom after years of poor management by Gottfried Walbaum. Saratogians would continue to worry about summer racing during the next two decades. This was not missed by the *Saratogian* in its opening day edition, which mentioned "unauthorized" reports on its editorial page that the 1946 season would be the last in the Spa city. The Saratoga Association assured Spa fans the meet would not be moved.

The main track played fast for much of the meet, with several records equaled or exceeded. Lucky Draw set a new track record of 1:55 2/5 for a mile and three-sixteenths in the Merchants' and

Citizens' Handicap on August 15. And he set a new track record on August 24 in the Saratoga Handicap. He was timed in 2:01 3/5 for 10 furlongs. It was better than the 2:01 4/5 recorded by Sir Barton in the same race in 1920, a year in which Man o' War recorded the same time in the Travers Stakes. Also on August 24, Blue Border set a new track record of 1:09 3/5 for 6 furlongs in the Grand Union Hotel Stakes. One week later, Blue Border would equal the track record of 1:17 for 6 ½ furlongs in the Hopeful Stakes.

Saratogian Ernie Lloyd, who served in World War II, recalled this period in an interview with the author. Lloyd said one of the reasons for the speed records was the storage of military equipment on the main track during 1943-45, when Saratoga's race dates were conducted at Belmont Park. According to Lloyd, much of the track cushion had been pressed down by the equipment, leaving only one inch or so above the base.

Lloyd also spoke of the walking of horses from the train depot on West Circular Street to the track in the 1930's. He said a common fee for the walkers, unemployed "street people" from the west side of the city during the Great Depression, was one dollar for the walk along Lincoln Avenue and Crescent Street on dirt horse paths to the track.[1]

John Mangona, who served as Resident Manager of Saratoga

Race Course during a career of nearly a half-century at the track, echoed the sentiments of Lloyd regarding the post-war period. Mangona first came to the track in 1948 with the firm of S. A. Scullen of nearby Waterford, which the Saratoga Association contracted for maintenance of the track, buildings and grounds. Mangona remembered seeing cots and tents left over from military storage, and agreed with Lloyd on his recollection of the fast times in 1946.[2]

Mangona joined the Greater New York Association, which later became the New York Racing Association, in 1959 at the invitation of Resident Manager Ed McDermott. He retired in 1996 after a career that saw him work on resurfacing of the main track in 1959, with new drainage and a ten-inch clay base; building of the main track turf courses in 1961-62; building of the Oklahoma Training Track turf course; the steeplechase training area at the Oklahoma; and building of a one-mile chute on the Oklahoma.

Significantly, when racing returned to Saratoga after the second World War, a dozen of its previous race days upstate remained downstate, this time at Jamaica. The "Saratoga at Jamaica" statistics during this period strengthened the arguments of those who did not want Saratoga Springs to have exclusive summer dates. The situation was not helped by a new Saratoga County pari-mutuel tax of 5 percent. While Saratoga Race Course recorded its first million-dollar betting day on August 10, 1946, the Spa was no match for Jamaica. In 1946, for example, the betting for four weeks at Saratoga was $21,249,207; at Jamaica it was $24,850,699 for just two weeks. The Saratoga Association, though, remained loyal to its namesake, and the profits made at Jamaica enabled it to keep purses healthy enough upstate to ensure high quality racing.

The tax drew opposition from the City of Saratoga Springs, with Mayor Addison Mallery predicting it would threaten the future of racing at the Spa. City leaders pleaded for a reduction to 2.5 percent, and noted, correctly as it turned out, that nearby states such as New Jersey and Rhode Island would benefit because they did not have a local pari-mutuel tax.

This was the era of Gallorette, one of the greatest race mares of all time. In 1947 at Saratoga, she captured the Wilson Mile at Saratoga and lost the Whitney and Saratoga handicaps by a head and neck, respectively. The following year she won her second Wilson Mile, and captured the Whitney Handicap. During her career of 72 starts, Gallorette started against the opposite sex 55 times. A member of the Hall of Fame, she defeated her own sex in races such as the Acorn, Pimlico Oaks, Delaware Oaks, and Beldame.

Also winning at Saratoga in 1947 was one of the turf giants of the 20th century, E. P. Taylor of Canada. His filly Spats won the

THE SARATOGA ASSOCIATION
FOR THE IMPROVEMENT OF THE BREED OF HORSES
6 AND 8 EAST 46TH STREET
NEW YORK

Schuylerville Stakes. Taylor would go on to remake Canadian racing by building the new Woodbine at Toronto in 1956. He bred dozens of champions who won titles in North America and Europe. On the Taylor list are greats such as Northern Dancer, Nijinsky II, Glorious Song, Nearctic, Try My Best, Storm Bird, and El Gran Senor.

When the Sanford Stud won the Whitney Handicap with Round View in 1949, it was a reminder of past glories at Stephen Sanford's beloved Saratoga. He was trained by Hollie Hughes, who had been associated with the Sanfords for more than 70 years, having first worked at Hurricana Stud in 1903. Hughes, elected to the Hall of Fame in 1973, won his first race at Saratoga in 1914 as a trainer, and conditioned the Sanford stock for Stephen Sanford's son John, and grandson Stephen.

The National Museum of Racing

Another highlight of Saratoga in the post-War years was the creation of a new institution dedicated to the history of the sport. Founders of the National Museum of Racing gathered at the track in 1950 to discuss the project, which had been promoted and sponsored by the Saratoga Springs Chamber of Commerce. Among those meeting were Saratoga Association president F. S. von Stade, George D. Widener, Donald P. Ross, Carlton F. Burke, Charles S.

Strub, S. Bryce Wing, and Maj. Louie A. Beard. Mayor Addison Mallery offered the Canfield Casino, in downtown Congress Park, as a site for the new organization, and it was housed there until the construction of the permanent home on Union Avenue in 1955. The formal opening, attended by thousands, was on August 6, 1951, at the Canfield Casino. The first donation to the National Museum of Racing was a shoe worn by Kentucky, winner of the first Travers Stakes in 1864. The formal dedication of the present building on Union Avenue was on August 16, 1955, and the National Museum of Racing opened to the public on June 2, 1956.

Tom Fool

Tom Fool, one of the true greats of an outstanding collection of thoroughbreds in the 1950's, was a two-year-old at Saratoga in 1951. The Greentree Stable runner, bred by Duval A. Headley, won at first asking on August 13. He followed with wins in the Sanford on August 20 and the Grand Union Hotel on August 25. In the latter he defeated Alfred G. Vanderbilt's Cousin, who up to that point had won all five of his starts including the Great American at Aqueduct and the Flash Stakes at Saratoga. Cousin turned the tables on Tom Fool in the Hopeful Stakes on September 1, but the Greentree runner would go on to capture the juvenile championship with

THE SARATOGA ASSOCIATION
FOR THE IMPROVEMENT OF THE BREED OF HORSES
6 AND 8 EAST 46TH STREET
NEW YORK

Tom Fool won the Wilson and Whitney at Saratoga in 1953.

victories in the Futurity at Belmont and the East View at Jamaica.

Tom Fool missed the classics at age 3 in 1952, due to a fever and cough which followed a neck loss in the Wood Memorial. His somewhat uneven campaign that year included a victory over older horses in the Wilson Mile on August 5, and a third in the Travers on August 16 as the favorite. Tom Fool secured no titles that year, but returned in 1953 to stage one of the greatest campaigns in history by an older horse.

In short, Tom Fool was unbeaten in ten starts as a four-year-old, meeting all comers while carrying top weights at distances from 5 ½ furlongs to a mile and a quarter. He won the Metropolitan on May 23 under 130 pounds at Belmont, the Suburban one week later under 128 pounds at 1 ¼ miles, the 7-furlong Carter under 135 pounds in 1:22 on June 27 at Aqueduct, and the Brooklyn on July 11 at Aqueduct under 136 pounds at 1 ¼ miles. The Metropolitan, Suburban and Brooklyn comprise the New York handicap triple crown, a series that received high respect for decades in the 20th century. Tom Fool was only the second to have won it, the first being Whisk Broom II in 1913. Tom Fool went on to sweep the Wilson and Whitney at Saratoga, and completed his season and career in the Sysonby at Belmont Park and the Pimlico Special, earning Horse of the Year honors.

Tom Fool retired with earnings of $570,165, with a record of 21-7-1 from 30 starts, and then went on to accomplish another thoroughbred rarity in siring a horse of his own stature in the great Buckpasser. That immortal Phipps runner was out of the mare Busanda, the daughter of War Admiral who won the first of her two consecutive Saratoga Cups at Saratoga in Tom Fool's juvenile season of 1951.

Native Dancer

Following Tom Fool's juvenile season of 1951, another racing immortal laid down a phenomenal record at the Spa as a youngster in 1952. Native Dancer was unstoppable that summer, winning four stakes races in the space of 26 days. Bred and owned by Alfred G. Vanderbilt, he won the Flash, Saratoga Special, Grand Union Hotel and Hopeful from August 4 to August 30. Native Dancer lost only the Kentucky Derby in a career of 22 starts, finishing a mere head from perfection. He returned to Saratoga in 1953 to win the Travers Stakes at odds of 1-to-20, and once more as a four-year-old in the Oneonta Handicap. He won the Oneonta, an exhibition under 137 pounds, by nine lengths in a prep for the Whitney Handicap. Old foot problems returned in the Oneonta, and Vanderbilt decided to retire Native Dancer.

He retired with earnings of $785,240, with a record of 21-1-0 in 22 starts. He was a unanimous champion as a two-year-old, also earning Horse of the Year honors in the Thoroughbred Racing Association poll. Native Dancer was also champion three-year-old in 1953, and in 1954 was Horse of the Year despite a limited campaign of just three starts. He also made a tremendous mark at stud through his son Raise A Native and daughter Natalma.

Nashua and Needles

The final two editions of the Hopeful Stakes conducted by the Saratoga Association were won by juveniles destined for the Hall of Fame, Nashua and Needles.

The first was Belair Stud's Nashua, whose victory on August 28, 1954, followed by one week his score in the Grand Union Hotel Stakes. Over the next two campaigns, Nashua went on to win many of the jewels of New York racing, such as the Wood Memorial, Belmont and Dwyer stakes, Jockey Club Gold Cup, and Suburban Handicap. He did not race at Saratoga following his two-year-old campaign. Nashua, however, trained at Saratoga in 1955 under the guidance of trainer "Sunny Jim" Fitzsimmons for his match race that summer against Swaps, to whom he had finished second in the Kentucky Derby. The $100,000 Washington Park Match took place on August 31, with Nashua leading all the way to win by 6 ½ lengths at a mile and a quarter.

In volume one of his work *Legacies of the Turf – A Century of Great Thoroughbred Breeders,* historian Ed Bowen relates that William Woodward Sr. respected stamina in the thoroughbred more than any other trait.[3] Thus, it is no surprise that his Belair Stud had four winners of the ten-furlong Travers Stakes in Little Chief (1922), Petee-Wrack (1928), Granville (1936), and Fenelon (1940). The first two were bred by Belair and raced, respectively, by Rancocas Stable and J. R. Macomber. Nor is it surprising that Belair won four editions of the 14-furlong Saratoga Cup with Gallant Fox (1930), Granville (1936), Isolater (1939) and Fenelon (1940). Isolater and Fenelon ran one-two in 1940 in a non-betting edition of the Saratoga Cup, essentially a walkover for the Belair entry.

Belair Stud also won five editions of the historic Alabama Stakes at Saratoga, the 10-furlong filly classic first run in 1872. They were Priscilla Ruley (1924), Vagrancy (1942), Vienna (1944), Hypnotic (1946) and Sabette (1953). The win by Vienna came at Belmont Park. Runners from Belair Stud also won the Schuylerville, Diana, Whitney, Test, Saratoga Special, Spinaway and Saranac.

Needles made a single appearance at Saratoga during his career, in the Hopeful Stakes on August 27, 1955. He won as he pleased by

3 ½ lengths over Career Boy, a future champion on turf.

An Historic Alabama Stakes

During the final week of the 1955 season, the Alabama Stakes was won by Rico Reto. She defeated seven rivals, who comprised an extraordinary example of the quality associated with the historic race for three-year-old fillies. Finishing second was Rokeby Stable's Blue Banner, who had earlier won the Test Stakes and would later capture the Distaff and Firenze. Blue Banner became the dam of Key Bridge, who in turn produced Horse of the Year Fort Marcy and three-year-old champion Key to the Mint.

Third in the Alabama of 1955 was Wheatley Stable's Misty Morn, who would go on to be champion three-year-old filly with wins in the Monmouth Oaks, Diana Handicap, and Gallant Fox, the last at 1 5/8 miles over males including that year's Travers winner Thinking Cap. Misty Morn produced champion juvenile males Bold Lad and Successor.

Fourth in the Alabama was Cain Hoy Stable's Lalun, the dam of Never Bend and Bold Reason. The brilliant Never Bend was champion juvenile male of 1962 when he won the Futurity, Cowdin and Champagne in succession. He would go on to be a top sire. Bold Reason won the Travers Stakes in 1971.

A track program in 1955, the final year of the Saratoga Association.

95

Sixth in the Alabama of 1955 was Brookmeade Stable's Flower Bowl. She became the mother of Hall of Fame female Bowl of Flowers, winner of the Coaching Club American Oaks. Flower Bowl also produced stakes winners and full brothers Graustark and His Majesty, both outstanding sires.

Finally, the seventh-place finisher in this edition of the Alabama Stakes was Wheatley Stable's High Voltage, the previous year's champion two-year-old filly by virtue of wins in the Matron and Selima stakes. High Voltage went on to become the dam of champion sprinter Impressive, winner of the Fall Highweight, Quaker City and Sport Page handicaps. High Voltage also produced major stakes winners Bold Commander and Great Power.

This was the Saratoga Association's final year of ownership of Saratoga Race Course, ending 90 years of stewardship of the famous track.

A NEW ORDER FOR NEW YORK RACING

Despite its glorious traditions, Saratoga Race Course was far down the list of the nation's tracks in terms of purses in the post-World War II era. While New York State as a whole ranked first or second with California during this period, Saratoga could not even crack the top ten of individual tracks with regard to purse payouts.

Suffolk Downs, in Boston, for example, regularly ranked above Saratoga Race Course, as did Garden State and Monmouth Park in New Jersey.[4]

For the period 1946-50, in terms of purses, Saratoga never ranked higher than 13th in the nation. While it figures that Hollywood Park, Santa Anita, Belmont and Aqueduct would be richer than Saratoga at this time, it might surprise contemporary readers that Suffolk Downs, Bay Meadows, and Detroit Race Course also ranked above the Spa. In the late 20th century, and on into the 21st century, purses at Saratoga Race Course were often the highest in the United States.

Further, states like New Jersey and Illinois were strengthening their positions relative to New York, whose facilities were aging and overdue for major refurbishment. The oldest was Saratoga, where organized thoroughbred racing began at the Saratoga Trotting Course in 1863 and moved across Union Avenue in Saratoga Springs to its permanent location in 1864. It was owned by the Saratoga Association. Aqueduct, owned by the Queens County Jockey Club, opened in 1894. Jamaica, owned by the Metropolitan Jockey Club, opened in 1903, while Belmont Park, owned by the Westchester Racing Association, opened in 1905.

All four tracks were in private hands, and its members could not handle the cost of improvements with the amount of pari-mutuel handle allotted to their associations by the state. The tax in New York, that is, the amount of money taken from the betting pools by the state that is set by law, was larger than most other states with racing. New York tracks in 1954 and 1955 were receiving 4 per cent as their allotment from the pari-mutuel tax charged in the state. However, for those same two years, New Jersey tracks were receiving 6 per cent and Rhode Island tracks were receiving 6 ½ per cent as their allotment from the pari-mutuel tax in their states.

With a state Joint Legislative Task Force in 1951 having outlined the situation, the time was ripe for state racing and political leaders to restructure the state industry.

The Jockey Club appointed a special committee which proposed a solution that did not change the pari-mutuel tax schedule, or require the state to lend any credit. The committee members were John W. Hanes as chairman, plus James Cox Brady, Christopher T. Chenery, Harry F. Guggenheim, John Hay Whitney, and George D. Widener, chairman of The Jockey Club. They proposed the Greater New York Association, a non-profit organization that could neither pay dividends on its stock nor transfer any of its assets to stockholders upon liquidation. The GNYA would acquire the four tracks, with the ultimate goal of closing either Aqueduct or Jamaica, completely rebuilding Belmont Park, and improving Saratoga. The plan also called for a franchise, or an enforceable contract, with New York which would end the annual application for racing licenses and simultaneously allow the GNYA to borrow money with its existence secured on a long-term basis.[5]

The 25-year plan was considered sufficient time to repay debt incurred by the GNYA for the acquisition and improvement of the track properties. The Jockey Club plan held that the pari-mutuel tax schedule could be preserved, with a view to actually increasing revenue to New York through modernized facilities, resulting in a revival of the sport that would produce better racing and higher betting handles, hence increasing a return to the state. Legislative, industry, and public discussion on the The Jockey Club plan began early in the 1955 legislative session in New York. Legislation was needed to set up the GNYA, which would obtain exclusive racing at its member tracks. Key provisions included a right of franchise revocation on the part of the state, as well as the transfer of all GNYA assets to the New York State Governor upon termination of its existence.

On February 11, 1955, New York State Director of the Budget Paul H. Appleby argued against the plan in a memorandum to Daniel Gutman, counsel to Governor Averell Harriman. In his view, the state was allowing – indeed guaranteeing – the owners of Aqueduct,

Belmont, Jamaica and Saratoga a way to get out from under their financial obligations with the creation of GNYA. Mr. Appleby worried that the state was going to be underwriting future operations of the GNYA, and wrote, "I think there are more deserving types of activity which could be given state sponsorship."[6]

Soon thereafter, The Jockey Club proposed changes that included state approval of vacancies on the GNYA board, state approval of the acquisition of the racing facilities, and a limit of 25 years on the franchise.

On April 4, 1955, Ashley Trimble Cole, chairman of the New York State Racing Commission, outlined what the commission would require of the GNYA in a letter to Governor Harriman. Chairman Cole assured the governor that the commission had the financial reports of the four tracks as of December 31, 1954, which would provide information on their value. Chairman Cole also said the commission required plans for the merger of the tracks into the GNYA, as well as plans for refurbishments and construction. He also noted the commission would continue to require application for racing dates.[7]

Cole, in a speech to The Jockey Club at Saratoga in 1953, had promoted the idea of revitalizing New York racing, citing the competition in other states with more modern facilities.

THE SARATOGA ASSOCIATION
FOR THE IMPROVEMENT OF THE BREED OF HORSES
6 AND 8 EAST 46TH STREET
NEW YORK

One week later, on April 11, 1955, the Conference of Mayors and Other Municipal Officials weighed in against The Jockey Club Plan. In a memorandum signed by Morgan Strong, executive secretary, the group objected that GNYA discussions were taking place without input from the cities which hosted the tracks. The organization included Saratoga Springs Mayor Addison Mallery.[8]

The State Department of Taxation and Finance, on April 12, 1955, came out against the plan. In a detailed accounting of how current taxable income was paid by the four tracks, Commissioner George M. Braglani reviewed the different method of tax collection the new law would require of the non-profit GNYA. He acknowledged the proposed $1,000 daily franchise fee was an accurate one, but suggested concerns about whether or not the number of racing dates might change under the new format. Commissioner Braglani also said the proposed legislation did not address the collection and administration of the tax.[9]

The Association of the Bar of the City of New York, on April 14, 1955, wrote Counsel Gutman its review of the proposed legislation. The bar association found only one objection, namely the aforementioned issue of collecting the franchise fee. While taking no position on whether or not Governor Harriman should sign the bill, the bar association said the issue of franchise fee collection did not

THE SARATOGA ASSOCIATION
FOR THE IMPROVEMENT OF THE BREED OF HORSES
6 AND 8 EAST 46TH STREET
NEW YORK

warrant a veto.[10]

Complaints against The Jockey Club plan also came from people within the New York racing community. Leading trainer Max Hirsch wired Governor Harriman, calling the plan to rebuild Belmont "foolish," and warned that the Metropolitan area needed three tracks, thus arguing against the closure of either Aqueduct or Jamaica.[11]

Isidor Bieber wrote Governor Harriman on April 18, 1955, expressing anger at the plan to close Jamaica, saying 40,000 people attended the races the previous Saturday.[12] Several days later, Bieber wrote Counsel Gutman, asking him to consider whether or not New York should tie itself up for 25 years, and wondered if a future governor could undo the franchise. A leading owner and breeder of his generation, he was co-owner of the Bieber-Jacobs Stable and co-bred greats like Hail to Reason, Affectionately, Allez France and Straight Deal.

Attorney Jerome J. Fendrick, also a horse owner and legal counsel to the New York Horsemen's Benevolent and Protective Association, came out against the plan in a letter to Counsel Gutman on April 25, 1955. He argued the plan would actually help New Jersey, as the closure of one of the Metropolitan tracks would reduce stall space for New York horsemen. Fendrick also mentioned the popularity of frequent changes of venue at Aqueduct, Belmont and Jamaica, saying longer meetings at each track would gradually prove unpopular with fans.[13]

In a lengthy letter to Governor Harriman, the Queens County Jockey Club, owners of Aqueduct, came out against the plan in its existing form and urged further study. Noting that the presidents of Belmont, Jamaica and Saratoga were members of The Jockey Club, while the QCJC president was not, the club said cost estimates for purchasing and refurbishing the tracks were vastly underestimated. The QCJC letter also said that the success of neighboring states was due to lower pari-mutuel taxes than those levied by New York. The Queens County letter also said The Jockey Club had no experience in running tracks, and that racing as a private, for-profit enterprise, had been successful.[14]

The Jockey Club Plan received a major assist from New York State Attorney General Jacob K. Javits on April 22, 1955, when he wrote Governor Harriman that he found no legal objection to the bill. Governor Harriman signed the legislation into law on April 29, 1955, after it was approved in close votes by both houses of the New York State legislature. The Assembly vote was 77-63, while the Senate vote was 31-23. The respective minimum yeas in each house were 70 and 30.

Within a few months, the GNYA began the process of acquiring

THE SARATOGA ASSOCIATION
FOR THE IMPROVEMENT OF THE BREED OF HORSES
6 AND 8 EAST 46TH STREET
NEW YORK

the tracks of Aqueduct, Belmont, Jamaica, and Saratoga from their owners for approximately $20 million. A total of 31,661 shares in the Saratoga Association were valued at $102.50 per share. Stockholders in the Saratoga Association were notified in July, 1955, of the offer.[15] Among the larger stockholders in the Saratoga Association were George D. Widener, Francis Skiddy von Stade, C. V. Whitney, H. F. Sinclair, Harry M. Stevens, Inc., and John A. Morris.

On April 10, 1958, the GNYA was renamed the New York Racing Association. According to NYRA president John Hanes, the previous name was confusing to the general public, which often thought it referred to the five boroughs of New York City. Hanes also said the old name tended to cause people to think it conducted racing only downstate and not at Saratoga.[16]

The stock of the GNYA, and subsequently the New York Racing Association, at $50 par value, could be purchased by and sold only to a duly approved new trustee taking the seat of a prior trustee.

As feared by Hirsch, Jamaica Race Track conducted its last meeting in 1959, closing its doors after the final card on August 1 that summer. NYRA sold the track and it became the Rochdale Park housing development. Races such as the Wood Memorial and Gotham Stakes, which had been conducted there since their respective inaugurals in 1925 and 1953, were moved to Aqueduct.

A Sesquicentennial Celebration

The New York Racing Association guided the fortunes of Saratoga Race Course in the decades following its acquisition from the Saratoga Association. Organized thoroughbred racing in Saratoga Springs celebrates its 150th anniversary in 2013, an accomplishment marked by Saratoga Race Course surpassing Aqueduct and Belmont in terms of attendance and betting handle in the final decades of the 20th century. Few racing experts in 1955 would have predicted such a dramatic development.

The growth of Saratoga in those terms led to a gradual decrease in the days raced downstate during summer, with a corresponding increase upstate. When racing returned to Saratoga following three years at Belmont Park (1943, 1944, 1945) in World War II, the Saratoga Association allotted 24 days of sport at the upstate track. That was the number of race days at Saratoga from 1946 until 1991, save for an odd season in 1982 of 27 consecutive days. The meeting increased to 30 days in 1991, to 36 days in 1997, and reached 40 days in 2010, equaling the old record of 40 days in 1882.

One of the most important developments at Saratoga Race Course in the late 20th century occurred in 1980 when the New York Racing Association opened the Oklahoma Training Track for training in spring and fall. Several hundred horses are on the

THE SARATOGA ASSOCIATION
FOR THE IMPROVEMENT OF THE BREED OF HORSES
6 AND 8 EAST 46TH STREET
NEW YORK

grounds from April to November each year, enjoying the benefits of a peaceful setting and a training track that many horsemen consider one of the best in the United States. Those horsemen have purchased homes upstate, and commute from Saratoga Springs to Aqueduct and Belmont during the months of training at the Oklahoma.

For much of Saratoga's thoroughbred history, the owners, trainers, and racehorses were only visitors each summer for the racing season. Now, they live here, at the summit of champions.

THE SARATOGA ASSOCIATION
FOR THE IMPROVEMENT OF THE BREED OF HORSES
6 AND 8 EAST 46TH STREET
NEW YORK

A contemporary view of the Oklahoma Training Track.

THE SARATOGA ASSOCIATION
FOR THE IMPROVEMENT OF THE BREED OF HORSES
6 AND 8 EAST 46TH STREET
NEW YORK

Appendix A
RACING DATES AT SARATOGA RACE COURSE 1901-1955

YEAR	NO. OF DAYS	CALENDAR DATES
1901	22	August 5-29
1902	22	August 4-28
1903	22	August 3-27
1904	22	August 1-25
1905	22	July 31 - August 24
1906	22	August 6-30
1907	22	August 5-29
1908	15	July 30 - August 16
1909	24	August 2-28
1910	24	August 4-31
1911	0	
1912	0	
1913	26	August 2 - September 1
1914	25	August 1-29
1915	24	August 2-28
1916	24	July 31 - August 26
1917	26	August 1-30
1918	27	August 1-31
1919	26	August 1-30

THE SARATOGA ASSOCIATION
FOR THE IMPROVEMENT OF THE BREED OF HORSES
6 AND 8 EAST 46TH STREET
NEW YORK

1920	26	August 2-31
1921	27	August 1-31
1922	27	August 1-31
1923	26	July 31 - August 30
1924	26	August 1-30
1925	26	July 31 - August 29
1926	26	July 30 - August 28
1927	30	August 1 - September 3
1928	30	July 30 - September 1
1929	30	July 29 - August 31
1930	28	July 30 - August 30
1931	27	August 6 - September 5
1932	30	August 1 - September 3
1933	27	August 3 - September 2
1934	30	July 30 - September 1
1935	30	July 29 - August 31
1936	28	July 29 - August 29
1937	30	July 26 - August 28
1938	30	July 25 - August 27
1939	30	July 31 - September 2
1940	30	July 29 - August 31
1941	30	July 28 - August 30
1942	30	July 27 - August 29
1943	30	July 26 - August 28*
1944	30	July 31 - September 2*
1945	24	August 6 - September 1*

THE SARATOGA ASSOCIATION
FOR THE IMPROVEMENT OF THE BREED OF HORSES
6 AND 8 EAST 46TH STREET
NEW YORK

Year	Days	Dates
1946	12	July 22 - August 3**
	24	August 5-31
1947	12	July 21 - August 2**
	24	August 4-30
1948	12	July 19 - July 31**
	24	August 2-28
1949	12	July 18 - July 30**
	24	August 1-27
1950	12	July 17 - July 29**
	24	July 31 - August 26
1951	12	July 23 - August 4**
	24	August 6 - September 1
1952	12	July 21 - August 2**
	24	August 4-30
1953	12	July 20 - August 1**
	24	August 3-29
1954	18	July 12-31**
	24	August 2-28
1955	18	July 11-30**
	24	August 1-27

NOTES: No racing at Saratoga in 1911 and 1912 due to a legislative ban on gambling.

*Races conducted at Belmont Park during the World War II years of 1943-1945.

**Races conducted at Jamaica Race Track.

THE SARATOGA ASSOCIATION
FOR THE IMPROVEMENT OF THE BREED OF HORSES
6 AND 8 EAST 46TH STREET
NEW YORK

Appendix B
TRIVIA

... The unusual occurrence of a major dirt race being transferred to turf happened at Saratoga on August 4, 1903. The main track was considered so bad that the Alabama Stakes was run on the new turf course. The winner had the interesting name of Stamping Ground.

... A short-lived Saratoga Derby was raced in 1904, 1905 and 1906, won respectively by Delhi, Cairngorm and Accountant.

... Origins of the Reading Room date to at least 1910. The *Saratogian* on July 15 reported that Saratoga Association president Richard T. Wilson revealed for the first time a "reading room" social club similar to those in Newport and Bar Harbor. Accordingly, the SA rented two cottages at the Grand Union Hotel for the 1910 meet, calling them "The Reading Room."

... For periods of time throughout its history, the Saratoga infield has been available for fans. In 1905, admission to the infield was one dollar. There were a reported 5,000 fans in the infield for Man o' War's victory in the Travers on August 21, 1920.

THE SARATOGA ASSOCIATION
FOR THE IMPROVEMENT OF THE BREED OF HORSES
6 AND 8 EAST 46TH STREET
NEW YORK

. . . The infield lake at Saratoga Race Course came about during the building of a new main track in 1917. The hole created by the removal of top soil and clay for the surface was filled with water, and the lake was part of the grounds in 1918.

. . . Jockey Laverne Fator's win total during the 1921 Saratoga meeting is one of the best in history. The 27-day meet had six races daily, for a total of 162 events. Fator won 38 races, or slightly more than 23 percent of them. He was a member of the inaugural class of inductees into the National Museum of Racing and Hall of Fame in 1955.

. . . Seldom is a championship secured as early as late June, but that was the case with the sensational two-year-old Dice in 1927. Bred by Harry Payne Whitney and owned by the Wheatley Stable, he was unbeaten in five starts through the Great American Stakes at Aqueduct on June 23, in which he carried 130 pounds. Sadly, on August 12 at Saratoga he died of a hemorrhage of the lungs following morning exercise.

. . . Exhibition races were held at the Oklahoma Training Track on July 4, 1943, sponsored by the Saratoga Association and Greentree Stable. The Saratoga summer meeting that year was run at Belmont Park.

Appendix C
STAKES WINNERS OF 1901-1955 AT SARATOGA RACE COURSE

There was no racing at Saratoga during a legislative blackout in 1911 and 1912, and again in 1943, 1944 and 1945 when the dates were transferred to Belmont Park during World War II.

This list is not all inclusive for the period, but rather of the major stakes of the time. Some, such as the Grand Union Hotel and United States Hotel, are no longer run.

ADIRONDACK STAKES

YEAR	WINNER	DIST.	TIME	OWNER
1901	Smart Set	6f	1:16 3/5	G. Walbaum
1902	Molly Brant	6f	1:13 1/5	S. Sanford
1903	Sweet Gretchen	6f	1:15 4/5	M. Hayman
1904	Broadcloth	6f	1:15 1/5	S. S. Brown
1905	Tangle	6f	1:13 2/5	F. Hitchcock
1906	Salvidere	6f	1:14 4/5	F. Hitchcock
1907	Beaucoup	6f	1:14	R. T. Wilson
1908	Sea Cliff	6f	1:15 1/5	H. P. Whitney
1909	Scarpia	6f	1:13	Chelsea Stable
1910	Zeus	6f	1:11 3/5	S. C. Hildreth

THE SARATOGA ASSOCIATION
FOR THE IMPROVEMENT OF THE BREED OF HORSES
6 AND 8 EAST 46TH STREET
NEW YORK

1913	Little Nephew	6f	1:15	M. B. Gruber
1914	Lady Barbary	6f	1:14 1/5	R. F. Carman
1915	Friar Rock	6f	1:17 4/5	A. Belmont
1916	Ultimatum	6f	1:14 4/5	S. Ross
1917	Happy Go Lucky	6f	1:13 3/5	H. P. Whitney
1918	Routledge	6f	1:12	Mrs. W. M. Jeffords
1919	Grayssian	6f	1:12 4/5	A. H. Diaz
1920	Exodus	6f	1:11 4/5	H. P. Whitney
1921	Oil Man	6f	1:11 4/5	Pelican Stable
1922	Cartoonist	6f	1:12	B. Fisher
1923	Elvina	6f	1:12	W. R. Coe
1924	Cloudland	6f	1:15	J. S. Cosden
1925	Blockhead	6f	1:13 3/5	Idle Hour Farm
1926	Friedjof Nansen	6f	1:14 3/5	Log Cabin Stud
1927	One Hour	6f	1:12	A. C. Schwartz
1928	The Worker	6f	1:15 2/5	Dorwood Stable
1929	War Saint	6f	1:12	G. D. Widener
1930	Ladana	6f	1:12	Rancocas Stable
1931	Brocado	6f	1:14	Mrs. J. H. Whitney
1932	Speed Boat	6f	1:12	Glen Riddle Farm
1933	Sun Celtic	6f	1:16	Fair Fields Stable
1934	Bud Flower	6f	1:15	E. R. Bradley
1935	Beanie M.	6f	1:13 4/5	E. R. Bradley
1936	Juliet W.	6f	1:13 3/5	B. Lissberger
1937	Creole Maid	6f	1:13 1/5	Mrs. W. M. Jeffords
1938	Matterhorn	6f	1:15	Wheatley Stable
1939	Rosetown	6f	1:13 3/5	G. D. Widener
1940	Tangled	6f	1:12	Greentree Stable

1941	Romping Home	6f	1:13 3/5	W. Ziegler Jr.
1942	La Reigh	6f	1:12 2/5	A. Pelleteri
1943	Fire Sticky	6f	1:10 4/5	G. Thorn
1944	Busher	6f	1:11 3/5	E. R. Bradley
1945	Rytina	6f	1:11	Mrs. W. P. Stewart
1946	Sweet Pegotty	6f	1:11 1/5	Mrs. E. D. Jacobs
1947	Inheritance	6f	1:11 4/5	Brookmeade Stable
1953	Riant	5.5f	1:05 2/5	Brookmeade Stable
1954	Hidden Ship	5.5f	1:05 4/5	Starr Ranch
1955	Dark Charger	5.5f	1:04 2/5	Mrs. H. W. Kellogg

NOTE: The Adirondack Stakes was not run in 1948, 1949, 1950, and 1952. In 1951, at Jamaica Race Track on Long Island, there was an Adirondack Handicap for fillies and mares, aged three years and older, at one mile. It was won by Greentree Stable's Ruddy in 1:38 2/5. From 1953-1955 it was run at Jamaica. Prior to 1946 it was run as a handicap.

ALABAMA STAKES

1901	Morningside	8.5f	1:47 4/5	W. C. Whitney
1902	Par Excellence	8.5f	1:47 3/5	Pepper Stable
1903	Stamping Ground	8.5T	1:56 4/5	F. R. Docter
1904	Beldame	9f	1:53 2/5	A. Belmont
1905	Tradition	10.5f	2:16 2/5	S. Paget
1906	Running Water	9f	1:52 2/5	Newcastle Stable
1907	Kennyetto	9f	1:54 1/5	J. Sanford
1908	Mayfield	9f	2:01	J. Sanford

THE SARATOGA ASSOCIATION
FOR THE IMPROVEMENT OF THE BREED OF HORSES
6 AND 8 EAST 46TH STREET
NEW YORK

1909	Maskette	9f	1:59 2/5	J. R. Keene
1910	Ocean Bound	9f	1:55	W. Clay
1913	Flying Fairy	9f	1:56 1/5	E. B. Cassatt
1914	Addie M.	9f	1:54 2/5	J. W. Messervy
1915	Waterblossom	9f	1:57 3/5	T. C. McDowell
1916	Malachite	9f	1:54 3/5	A. Belmont
1917	Sunbonnet	10f	2:07	A. K. Macomber
1918	Eyelid	10f	2:04 1/5	A. L. Aste
1919	Vexatious	10f	2:09 1/5	W. M. Jeffords
1920	Cleopatra	10f	2:07 4/5	W. R. Coe
1921	Prudery	10f	2:04 1/5	H. P. Whitney
1922	Nedna	10f	2:08	W. P. Thompson
1923	Untidy	10f	2:05 2/5	Greentree Stable
1924	Priscilla Ruley	10f	2:08 4/5	Belair Stud
1925	Maid at Arms	10f	2:07	Glen Riddle Farm
1926	Rapture	10f	2:06	H. P. Whitney
1927	Nimba	10f	2:06 4/5	M. Field
1928	Nixie	10f	2:10 1/5	Wheatley Stable
1929	Aquastella	10f	2:04 4/5	Mrs. F. A. Clark
1930	Escutcheon	10f	2:04 1/5	M. Field
1931	Risque	10f	2:05 3/5	Mrs. J. D. Hertz
1932	Top Flight	10f	2:06 2/5	C. V. Whitney
1933	Barn Swallow	10f	2:06 3/5	E. R. Bradley
1934	Hindu Queen	10f	2:05	M. L. Schwartz
1935	Alberta	10f	2:05 1/5	W. S. Kilmer
1936	Floradora	10f	2:06 2/5	E. D. Shaffer
1937	Regal Lily	10f	2:08 1/5	W. M. Jeffords
1938	Handcuff	10f	2:07 2/5	BrookmeadeStable

1939	War Plumage	10f	2:05	J. C. Brady
1940	Salaminia	10f	2:04 4/5	H. P. Headley
1941	War Hazard	10f	2:04 4/5	Glen Riddle Farm
1942	Vagrancy	10f	2:05 1/5	Belair Stud
1943	Stefanita	10f	2:04 2/5	G. D. Widener
1944	Vienna	10f	2:03 3/5	Belair Stud
1945	Sicily	10f	2:03 2/5	H. LaMontagne
1946	Hypnotic	10f	2:04 1/5	Belair Stud
1947	But Why Not	10f	2:05	King Ranch
1948	Compliance	10f	2:06	Lester Manor Stable
1949	Adile	10f	2:04	Mrs. W. M. Jeffords
1950	Busanda	10f	2:04 2/5	O. Phipps
1951	Kiss Me Kate	10f	2:05 3/5	W. M. Jeffords
1952	Lily White	10f	2:05 4/5	Mrs. W. M. Jeffords
1953	Sabette	10f	2:06	Belair Stud
1954	Parlo	10f	2:06	Foxcatcher Farm
1955	Rico Reto	10f	2:05 4/5	W. A. Hanger

NOTE: The 1903 Alabama was run on turf due to poor main track conditions.

ALBANY STAKES

1901	Dixieline	6f	1:13 4/5	R. T. Wilson Jr.
1902	Grey Friar	6f	1:12 3/5	F. R. Hitchcock
1903	Gold Saint	6f	1:15 2/5	J. P. Kramer
1904	Jack Lory	6f	1:14 2/5	J. W. Schorr
1905	James Reddick	6f	1:16 4/5	C. R. Ellison

1906	Eddie Ware	6f	1:16	M. H. Tichenor
1907	Jim Gaffney	6f	1:15 2/5	F. J. Farrell
1908	Sea Cliff	6f	1:17 4/5	H. P. Whitney
1909	Pretend	6f	1:16	T. Monahan
1910	Textile	6f	1:15 3/5	T. Monahan
1913	Bradley's Choice	6f	1:13	E. R. Bradley
1914	High Noon	6f	1:12 2/5	J. Butler
1915	Achievement	6f	1:17 4/5	R. F. Carman
1916	Crank	6f	1:13	S. Ross
1917	Sun Briar	6f	1:14 2/5	W. S. Kilmer
1918	Star Hampton	6f	1:12 1/5	W. M. Jeffords
1919	Kinnoul	6f	1:14 4/5	W. M. Jeffords
1920	Pahaska	6f	1:12	W. R. Coe
1921	Modo	6f	1:11	Modo Stable
1922	Zev	6f	1:15 3/5	Rancocas Stable
1923	Sunspero	6f	1:11 2/5	G. A. Cochran
1924	Nicholas	6f	1:15	F. J. Farrell
1925	Navigator	6f	1:15 1/5	Greentree Stable
1926	Sun Forward	6f	1:14 2/5	W. S. Kilmer
1927	Sledge Hammer	6f	1:13 2/5	G. A. Cochran
1928	Twink	6f	1:14 3/5	Loma Stable
1929	Peto	6f	1:14	Belair Stud
1930	Surf Board	6f	1:12 3/5	Greentree Stable
1931	Polonaise	6f	1:13	W. R. Coe
1932	Grand Time	6f	1:14 1/5	W. Ziegler Jr.
1933	Bazaar	6f	1:13	E. R. Bradley
1934	Bird Flower	6f	1:15 4/5	E. R. Bradley
1935	Sangreal	6f	1:12 4/5	Milky Way Farm

1936	Biologist	6f	1:13 2/5	E. R. Bradley
1937	Sky Larking	6f	1:12	Milky Way Farm
1938	Giles County	6f	1:12 4/5	Milky Way Farm
1939	Ramases	6f	1:12 1/5	H. P. Headley
1940	Zacharias	6f	1:12	Millsdale Stable
1941	Anytime	6f	1:13	G. D. Widener
1942	Very Snooty	6f	1:12 3/5	Brookmeade Stable
1943	Rodney Stone	6f	1:12	H. LaMontagne
1944	Plebiscite	6f	1:11 1/5	G. D. Widener
1945	Yesnow	6f	1:10 3/5	Mrs. A. Wichfield
1946	Donor	6f	1:10 2/5	D. Howe
1947	Peace of Mind	6f	1:12	Mill River Stable
1948	Noble Impulse	6f	1:12 3/5	C. Oglebay
1949	Detective	6f	1:12 2/5	Mrs. A. Wichfield
1950	Patch	6f	1:10 4/5	J. T. Taylor
1951	Hannibal	6f	1:12 4/5	B. Sharp
1952	Real Brother	6f	1:12 3/5	Mrs. G. F. Spear
1953	Quick Lunch	6f	1:11 4/5	Wheatley Stable
1954	Laugh	6f	1:12 1/5	Wheatley Stable
1955	Jean Baptiste	6f	1:12 2/5	Mrs. L. P. Tate

NOTE: The Albany was run at Jamaica from 1948-1955.

BEVERWYCK STEEPLECHASE

1901	The Bachelor	20f	6:34 2/5	T. Hitchcock
1902	Geo. W. Jenkins	20f	5:28 2/5	M. J. Maloney
1903	Lavator	20f	5:06	G. Tompkins

THE SARATOGA ASSOCIATION
FOR THE IMPROVEMENT OF THE BREED OF HORSES
6 AND 8 EAST 46TH STREET
NEW YORK

1904	Amur	20f	5:14 2/5	J. R. Colt
1905	Jimmy Lane	20f	5:31 3/5	Mr. Cotton
1906	Herculoid	20f	5:21	H. Craven
1907	McKittredge	20f	5:25	F. A. Clark
1908	Bayonet	20f	5:25 2/5	T. Hitchcock
1909	Sir Wooster	20f	5:22	Mr. Chetland
1910	Hylda	20f	5:30	F. A. Clark
1913	Postboy	16f	4:24	A. S. Cochran
1914	Savannah	16f	4:37	F. A. Clark
1915	Weldship	16f	4:21	E. M. Weld
1916	Weldship	16f	4:28	E. M. Weld
1917	Martian	16f	4:16	Glen Riddle Farm
1918	The Brook	16f	4:21 3/5	J. E. Griffith
1919	Hibler	16f	4:21 1/5	F. A. Clark
1920	Barklie	16f	4:22 1/5	W. M. Jeffords
1921	Syrdarya	16f	4:20	Dosoris Stable
1922	Bullseye	16f	4:24 2/5	J. S. Cosden
1923	Bullseye	16f	4:14 4/5	J. S. Cosden
1924	Houdini	16f	4:19 1/5	J. E. Widener
1925	Fredden Rock	16f	4:17 3/5	Brookmeade Stable
1926	Brightness	16f	4:16	Grassland Stable
1927	Laufjunge	16f	4:13 2/5	Log Cabin Stable
1928	Rabel	16f	4:18	J. Livingston
1929	Redbridge	16f	4:14 3/5	J. H. Macomber
1930	Personality	16f	4:21 4/5	V. Crane
1931	Bally Weaver	16f	4:19 3/5	Queen City Stable
1932	Barometer	16f	4:14	E. R. Bradley
1933	Crumpler	16f	4:20 4/5	Mrs. F. A. Clark

1934	Rocky Run	16f	4:08 3/5	Mrs. J. H. Whitney
1935	Red Flash	16f	4:18 3/5	F. A. Clark
1936	Rioter	16f	4:12	T. Hitchcock
1937	Jungle King	16f	4:15 3/5	Mrs. P. Whitney
1938	Gay Charles	16f	4:21	G. Whitney
1939	Whaddon Chase	16f	4:19 3/5	C. M. Kline
1940	Cottesmore	16f	4:17	G. H. Bostwick
1941	Ossabaw	16f	4:17 3/5	L. B. Mayer
1942	Invader	16f	4:15 3/5	Mrs. F. A. Clark
1943	Rouge Dragon	16f	3:46 3/5	M. A. Cushman
1944	Rouge Dragon	16f	3:48 1/5	M. A. Cushman
1945	War Battle	16f	3:49 4/5	K. Miller
1946	Rouge Dragon	16f	4:11 4/5	M. A. Cushman
1947	Floating Isle	16f	4:19 4/5	T. T. Mott
1948	The Heir	16f	4:15 1/5	Mrs. C. Sullivan
1949	Sun Bath	16f	4:20 1/5	R. W. Grant
1950	Pontius Pilate	16f	4:08 2/5	F. A. Clark
1951	Oedipus	16f	4:19 2/5	Mrs. O. Phipps
1952	His Boots	16f	4:09 1/5	Brookmeade Stable
1953	Sun Shower	16f	4:09 2/5	Mrs. G. V. Cardy
1954	King Commander	16f	4:08 3/5	L. R. Troiano
1955	Rythminhim	16f	4:22 2/5	Mrs. M. G. Walsh

DIANA HANDICAP

1939	War Regalia	9f	1:52 1/5	Mrs. W. M. Jeffords
1940	Piquet	9f	1:52	Greentree Stable
1941	Rosetown	9f	1:53 2/5	G. D. Widener

1942	Pomayya	9f	1:53	Brookmeade Stable
1943	Bonnet Ann	9f	1:50	Brookmeade Stable
1944	Whirlabout	9f	1:50 1/5	L. B. Mayer
1945	Surosa	9f	1:50 4/5	Foxcatcher Farms
1946	Miss Grillo	9f	1:50 1/5	Mill River Stable
1947	Miss Grillo	9f	1:50 2/5	Mill River Stable
1948	Carolyn A.	9f	1:51 4/5	B. F. Whitaker
1949	Spats	9f	1:52 2/5	Mrs. T. Christopher
1950	Ouija	9f	1:51 3/5	Brookmeade Stable
1951	Vulcania	9f	1:52 3/5	Belair Stud
1952	Busanda	9f	1:53 2/5	Ogden Phipps
1953	Sabette	9f	1:52 3/5	Belair Stud
1954	Lavender Hill	9f	1:52 3/5	Mrs. C. Silvers
1955	Misty Morn	9f	1:51 1/5	Wheatley Stable

FLASH STAKES

1901	Goldsmith	5f	1:01	W. C. Whitney
1902	Judith Campbell	5.5f	1:08	J. W. Schorr
1903	Tippecanoe	5.5f	1:08	H. M. Ziegler
1904	Sysonby	5.5f	1:06 4/5	J. R. Keene
1905	Burgomeister	5.5f	1:08 3/5	H. P. Whitney
1906	Peter Pan	5.5f	1:06 3/5	J. R. Keene
1907	Fair Play	5.5f	1:06 3/5	A. Belmont
1908	Edward	5.5f	1:07 4/5	J. E. Madden
1909	Waldo	5.5f	1:07	C. L. Harrison
1910	Semprolus	5.5f	1:09	R. F. Carman
1913	Old Rosebud	5.5f	1:07	H. C. Applegate

THE SARATOGA ASSOCIATION
FOR THE IMPROVEMENT OF THE BREED OF HORSES
6 AND 8 EAST 46TH STREET
NEW YORK

Year	Horse	Dist	Time	Owner
1914	Trial by Jury	5.5f	1:07	E. B. Cassatt
1915	Prince of Como	5.5f	1:10 1/5	G. A. Cochran
1916	Rickety	5.5f	1:07 4/5	H. P. Whitney
1917	Papp	5.5f	1:07 1/5	G. W. Loft
1918	Billy Kelly	5.5f	1:05 3/5	W. R. Coe
1919	Miss Jemima	5.5f	1:06 1/5	C. E. Rowe
1920	Moody	5.5f	1:05 4/5	H. P. Whitney
1921	Miss Joy	5.5f	1:06 2/5	Montfort Jones
1922	Dust Flower	5.5f	1:06	J. Milam
1923	Lord Baltimore	5.5f	1:08 3/5	W. Garth
1924	Felix	5.5f	1:07 3/5	G. D. Widener
1925	Sarmaticus	5.5f	1:06 4/5	R. L. Gerry
1926	Osmand	5.5f	1:08 2/5	J. E. Widener
1927	Distraction	5.5f	1:07 2/5	Wheatley Stable
1928	Jack High	5.5f	1:07 1/5	G. D. Widener
1929	Gallant Fox	5.5f	1:06	Belair Stud
1930	Jamestown	5.5f	1:06	G. D. Widener
1931	Irene's Bob	5.5f	1:06	J. E. Gaffney
1932	Happy Gal	5.5f	1:05 4/5	Belair Stud
1933	Elylee	5.5f	1:06 3/5	J. H. Loucheim
1934	Pitter Pat	5.5f	1:06 3/5	Belair Stud
1935	Red Rain	5.5f	1:07	C. V. Whitney
1936	Maedic	5.5f	1:06 3/5	Maemare Farm
1937	Maetall	5.5f	1:07 1/5	Maemare Farm
1938	Eight Thirty	5.5f	1:05 1/5	G. D. Widener
1939	Epatant	5.5f	1:06 1/5	Manhasset Stable
1940	Overdrawn	5.5f	1:05 1/5	G. D. Widener
1941	Ampitheatre	5.5f	1:06 1/5	Manhasset Stable

1942	Breezing Home	5.5f	1:06 1/5	W. Ziegler Jr.
1943	Tropea	5.5f	1:05	W. Helis
1944	Plebiscite	5.5f	1:04	G. D. Widener
1945	Assault	5.5f	1:04 4/5	King Ranch
1946	Gestapo	5.5f	1:05 3/5	Greentree Stable
1947	Star Bout	5.5f	1:05 1/5	Greentree Stable
1948	Algasir	5.5f	1:06 4/5	J. H. Skirvin
1949	Greek Ship	5.5f	1:07 1/5	Brookmeade Stable
1950	Northern Star	5.5f	1:05 1/5	Mrs. E. D. Weir
1951	Cousin	5.5f	1:06 1/5	A. G. Vanderbilt
1952	Native Dancer	5.5f	1:06	A. G. Vanderbilt
1953	Card Trick	5.5f	1:06 1/5	Greentree Stable
1954	Laugh	5.5f	1:07	Wheatley Stable
1955	Reneged	5.5f	1:05 1/5	Woodley Lane Fm.

GRAND UNION HOTEL STAKES

1901	King Hanover	6f	1:13 1/5	W. C. Whitney
1902	Grey Friar	6f	1:13	F. Hitchcock
1903	Highball	6f	1:14 1/5	W. Scheftel
1904	Siglight	6f	1:15	J. E. Madden
1905	Battleaxe	6f	1:14	H. P. Whitney
1906	Penarris	6f	1:13 3/5	F. O'Neill
1907	Colin	6f	1:13	J. R. Keene
1908	Edward	6f	1:15	J. E. Madden
1909	Chickasaw	6f	1:13 2/5	J. Caffrey
1910	Iron Mask	6f	1:12 4/5	J. R. Keene
1913	Black Broom	6f	1:13 1/5	H. P. Whitney

1914	Garbage	6f	1:13 3/5	E. B. Cassatt
1915	Puss N Boots	6f	1:13 3/5	F. P. Keene
1916	Hourless	6f	1:12 3/5	A. Belmont
1917	Sun Briar	6f	1:16 2/5	W. S. Kilmer
1918	Sweep On	6f	1:12 2/5	W. R. Coe
1919	Man o' War	6f	1:12	Glen Riddle Farm
1920	Prudery	6f	1:12	H. P. Whitney
1921	Kai-Sang	6f	1:12 3/5	Rancocas Stable
1922	Zev	6f	1:15	Rancocas Stable
1923	Big Blaze	6f	1:11 2/5	Glen Riddle Farm
1924	Sunsard	6f	1:15 4/5	W. S. Kilmer
1925	Haste	6f	1:12 1/5	J. E. Widener
1926	Kiev	6f	1:13	J. E. Widener
1927	Vito	6f	1:13	A. H. Cosden
1928	Twink	6f	1:16	Loma Stable
1929	Jim Dandy	6f	1:15 4/5	C. Earl
1930	Jamestown	6f	1:11 4/5	G. D. Widener
1931	Lucky Tom	6f	1:13	J. J. Robinson
1932	Ladysman	6f	1:11	W. R. Coe
1933	Roustabout	6f	1:15 2/5	C. V. Whitney
1934	Chance Sun	6f	1:14 2/5	J. E. Widener
1935	The Fighter	6f	1:12 3/5	Milky Way Farm
1936	Maedic	6f	1:14 1/5	Maemare Farm
1937	Fighting Fox	6f	1:12 2/5	Belair Stud
1938	No Competition	6f	1:12 1/5	Milky Way Farm
1939	Epatant	6f	1:14	Manhasset Stable
1940	New World	6f	1:11	A. G. Vanderbilt
1941	Shut Out	6f	1:12 1/5	Greentree Stable

1942	Devil's Thumb	6f	1:12 2/5	W. E. Boeing
1943	By Jiminy	6f	1:12 4/5	E. R. Bradley
1944	Pavot	6f	1:11 4/5	Greentree Stable
1945	Manipur	6f	1:11 4/5	J. M. Roebling
1946	Blue Border	6f	1:09 3/5	J. R. Bradley
1947	My Request	6f	1:11	B. F. Whitaker
1948	Magic Words	6f	1:11 4/5	Maine Chance Farm
1949	Suleiman	6f	1:12 3/5	Mrs. W.M. Jeffords
1950	Battle Morn	6f	1:13	Cain Hoy Stable
1951	Tom Fool	6f	1:11 4/5	Greentree Stable
1952	Native Dancer	6f	1:11 1/5	A. G. Vanderbilt
1953	Artismo	6f	1:12 3/5	J. C. Brady
1954	Nashua	6f	1:12 2/5	Belair Stud
1955	Career Boy	6f	1:12 2/5	C. V. Whitney

HOPEFUL STAKES

1903	Delhi	6f	1:13 1/5	J. R. Keene
1904	Tanya	6f	1:13 2/5	H. B. Duryea
1905	Mohawk II	6f	1:13 2/5	J. Sanford
1906	Peter Pan	6f	1:12	J. R. Keene
1907	Jim Gaffney	6f	1:15	F. Farrell
1908	Helmet	6f	1:12 1/5	J. R. Keene
1909	Rocky O'Brien	6f	1:13 1/5	J. McManus
1910	Novelty	6f	1:14	S. Hildreth
1913	Bringhurst	6f	1:12 2/5	J. N. Camden
1914	Regret	6f	1:16 2/5	H. P. Whitney
1915	Dominant	6f	1:13 4/5	L. S. Thompson

THE SARATOGA ASSOCIATION
FOR THE IMPROVEMENT OF THE BREED OF HORSES
6 AND 8 EAST 46TH STREET
NEW YORK

1916	Campfire	6f	1:14 3/5	R. T. Wilson
1917	Sun Briar	6f	1:15 3/5	W. S. Kilmer
1918	Eternal	6f	1:13 3/5	J. W. McClelland
1919	Man o' War	6f	1:13	Glen Riddle Farm
1920	Leonardo II	6f	1:12 2/5	J. W. McClelland
1921	Morvich	6f	1:12 3/5	B. Block
1922	Dunlin	6f	1:12 2/5	J. S. Cosden
1923	Diogenes	6f	1:12 3/5	Mrs. W. M. Jeffords
1924	Master Charlie	6f	1:13	W. Daniel
1925	Pompey	6.5f	1:17 4/5	Shoshone Stable
1926	Lord Chaucer	6.5f	1:19 4/5	Sagamore Stable
1927	Brooms	6.5f	1:20	Brookmeade Stable
1928	Jack High	6.5f	1:18 2/5	G. D. Widener
1929	Boojum	6.5f	1:17	H. P. Whitney
1930	Epithet	6.5f	1:17 3/5	G. A. Cochran
1931	Tick On	6.5f	1:20 2/5	Loma Stable
1932	Ladysman	6.5f	1:19 2/5	W. R. Coe
1933	Bazaar	6.5f	1:19	E. R. Bradley
1934	Psychic Bid	6.5f	1:18 4/5	Brookmeade Stable
1935	Red Rain	6.5f	1:19 4/5	C. V. Whitney
1936	Maedic	6.5f	1:20 1/5	Maemare Farm
1937	Sky Larking	6.5f	1:20 4/5	Milky Way Farm
1938	El Chico	6.5f	1:18 2/5	W. Ziegler Jr.
1939	Bimelech	6.5f	1:18 4/5	E. R. Bradley
1940	Whirlaway	6.5f	1:18	Calumet Farm
1941	Devil Diver	6.5f	1:18 3/5	Greentree Stable
1942	Devil's Thumb	6.5f	1:18 2/5	W. E. Boeing
1943	Bee Mac	6.5f	1:18 2/5	B. MacGuire

1944	Pavot	6.5f	1:18 4/5	W. M. Jeffords
1945	Star Pilot	6.5f	1:16 3/5	Maine Chance Farm
1946	Blue Border	6.5f	1:17	J. R. Bradley
1947	Relic	6.5f	1:17 2/5	Circle M Farm
1948	Blue Peter	6.5f	1:19 1/5	J. M. Roebling
1949	Middleground	6.5f	1:18 2/5	King Ranch
1950	Battlefield	6.5f	1:18	G. D. Widener
1951	Cousin	6.5f	1:19 1/5	A. G. Vanderbilt
1952	Native Dancer	6.5f	1:18 4/5	A. G. Vanderbilt
1953	Artismo	6.5f	1:18	J. C. Brady
1954	Nashua	6.5f	1:17 4/5	Belair Stud
1955	Needles	6.5f	1:18 1/5	D & H Stable

KENNER STAKES

1901	Baron Pepper	11f	2:21 4/5	Pepper Stable
1902	Lady Albercraft	10f	2:05 3/5	G. B. Morris
1903	Injunction	10f	2:07	J. R. Keene
1917	Omar Khayyam	9.5f	2:01 4/5	W. Viau
1918	Enfilado	9.5f	1:56 2/5	M. L. Schwartz
1919	Milkmaid	9.5f	1:56 4/5	J. K. L. Ross
1920	Man o' War	9.5f	1:56 3/5	S. D. Riddle
1921	Prudery	9.5f	1:57 3/5	H. P. Whitney
1922	Sweep By	9.5f	2:04 2/5	Mrs. A. R. Lawson
1923	Martingale	9.5f	1:59 4/5	J. S. Cosden
1924	Klondyke	9.5f	1:58 4/5	H. P. Whitney
1925	Stirrup Cup	9.5f	2:05	Greentree Stable
1926	Rock Star	9.5f	2:01 2/5	Brookmeade Stable

1927	Brown Bud	9.5f	1:59	F. Johnson
1928	Reigh Count	9.5f	1:59	Mrs. J. D. Hertz
1929	Marine	9.5f	1:59 2/5	J. E. Widener
1930	Whichone	9.5f	1:56 2/5	H. P. Whitney
1931	Mate	9.5f	1:58 1/5	A. C. Bostwick
1932	Dark Secret	9.5f	1:58 4/5	Wheatley Stable
1933	War Glory	9.5f	2:01 1/5	Glen Riddle Farm
1934	Discovery	9.5f	1:57 1/5	A. G. Vanderbilt
1935	St. Bernard	9.5f	2:00	E. D. Shaffer
1936	Granville	9.5f	1:58 3/5	Belair Stud
1937	Rex Flag	9.5f	1:58 2/5	Mrs. L. Viau
1938	Bull Lea	9.5f	1:57 4/5	Calumet Farm
1939	Hash	9.5f	1:58	Greentree Stable
1940	Your Chance	9.5f	1:58	Mrs. G. D. Widener
1941	War Relic	9.5f	1:58 2/5	Glen Riddle Farm
1942	Buckskin	9.5f	2:00	Greentree Stable

NOTE: First run in 1870, the Kenner was named in honor of Louisiana turf sportsman Duncan F. Kenner (1813-1887). He was a member of the Confederate Congress and a diplomat for the Confederate States of America. He developed an important racing stable as an owner and breeder at his Ashland Plantation near Donaldsonville, La. He raced at the famed Metairie Race Course in New Orleans, which he helped found in 1838. Kenner was also an organizer of the New Louisiana Jockey Club, which founded Fair Grounds Race Course in 1872. It was run as the Miller Stakes from 1920-1930, in honor of Andrew Miller, who owned Travers winners Roamer and Lady Rotha and who served as an officer of the Saratoga Association.

THE SARATOGA ASSOCIATION
FOR THE IMPROVEMENT OF THE BREED OF HORSES
6 AND 8 EAST 46TH STREET
NEW YORK

MERCHANTS' AND CITIZENS' HANDICAP

1901	Herbert	8.5f	1:50 1/5	W. C. Rollins
1902	Herbert	9f	1:56 2/5	W. C. Rollins
1903	Hermis	9f	1:51 3/5	E. R. Thomas
1904	Molly Brant	9f	1:51 3/5	J. Sanford
1905	Outcome	9.5f	2:02 3/5	W. Clay
1906	Redleaf	9.5f	2:02	J. O. Keene
1907	Running Water	9.5f	1:58 2/5	Newcastle Stable
1908	Dandelion	9.5f	1:58 4/5	T. Hitchcock
1909	Sir John Johnson	9.5f	1:58	Beverwyck Stable
1910	Sir John Johnson	9.5f	2:01 3/5	Beverwyck Stable
1913	Sam Jackson	9.5f	2:01 3/5	V. M. McGinnis
1914	Star Gaze	9.5f	2:03 4/5	H. L. Pratt
1915	Roamer	9.5f	1:59	A. Miller
1916	The Finn	9.5f	1:58	H. C. Hallenbeck
1917	Clematis II	9.5f	2:02 2/5	O. Lewisohn
1918	Midway	9.5f	1:57 1/5	J. W. Parrish
1919	Cudgel	9.5f	1:57 2/5	J. K. L. Ross
1920	Sir Barton	9.5f	1:55 3/5	J. K. L. Ross
1921	Exterminator	9.5f	1:57 2/5	W. S. Kilmer
1922	Devastation	9.5f	2:05	S. Pettit
1923	Bunting	9.5f	1:56 2/5	H. P. Whitney
1924	Sunsini	9.5f	2:05 1/5	Lilane Stable
1925	Spot Cash	9.5f	1:58	A. C. Bostwick
1926	Flagstaff	9.5f	1:59	La Brae Stable
1927	Chance Play	9.5f	1:59 1/5	Arden Farms
1928	Chance Shot	9.5f	2:03 1/5	J. E. Widener

THE SARATOGA ASSOCIATION
FOR THE IMPROVEMENT OF THE BREED OF HORSES
6 AND 8 EAST 46TH STREET
NEW YORK

1929	Petee-Wrack	9.5f	2:02 1/5	J. R. Macomber
1930	Frisius	9.5f	1:56 3/5	Belair Stud
1931	Curate	9.5f	2:02 4/5	J. E. Widener
1932	Reveille Boy	9.5f	1:59 1/5	J. A. Best
1933	Dark Secret	9.5f	1:57 2/5	Wheatley Stable
1934	Faireno	9.5f	1:58 3/5	Belair Stud
1935	Discovery	9.5f	1:57 2/5	A. G. Vanderbilt
1936	Esposa	9.5f	2:00 2/5	Middleburg Stable
1937	Count Arthur	9.5f	1:58	Mrs. J. D. Hertz
1938	Great Union	9.5f	1:57 2/5	Mrs. E. G. Lewis
1939	Sickle T.	9.5f	1:58 2/5	Mrs. B. F. Whitaker
1940	Isolater	9.5f	1:56 4/5	Belair Stud
1941	Fenelon	9.5f	1:58 4/5	Belair Stud
1942	Olympus	9.5f	1:58	Barrington Stable
1943	Lochinvar	9.5f	1:55	J. M. Roebling
1944	Princequillo	9.5f	1:55 1/5	Boone Hall Stable
1945	Coronal	9.5f	1:56 1/5	Dell Stable
1946	Lucky Draw	9.5f	1:55 2/5	G. D. Widener
1947	Loyal Legion	9.5f	1:58	W. M. Jeffords
	Talon (dh)			R. N. Ryan
1948	Beauchef	9.5f	1:59	Andes Stable
1949	Chains	9.5f	1:57 4/5	Brookmeade Stable
1950	My Request	9.5f	1:56 3/5	B. F. Whitaker
1951	County Delight	9.5f	1:57 2/5	Rokeby Stable
1952	Crafty Admiral	9.5f	1:57 2/5	Charfran Stable
1953	One Hitter	9.5f	1:56 3/5	Greentree Stable
1954	Capeador	9.5f	1:58	Brookmeade Stable
1955	First Aid	9.5f	1:58	Brookmeade Stable

NOTE: Run at Jamaica from 1948 to 1955.

THE SARATOGA ASSOCIATION
FOR THE IMPROVEMENT OF THE BREED OF HORSES
6 AND 8 EAST 46TH STREET
NEW YORK

NORTH AMERICAN STEEPLECHASE

1904	St. Jude	20f	5:14 2/5	Mr. Cotton
1905	Sandhurst	20f	5:28	J. W. Colt
1906	Alfar	20f	5:22	Bonnie Brook Stable
1907	Commodore Fontaine	24f	6:22	J. W. Colt
1908	Bat	24f	6:29	E. H. Carle
1909	Waterway	16f	4:22	Prospect Stable
1910	Aunt Jule	16f	4:26	Lexington Stable
1913	Wickson	16f	4:23	L. A. Ekers
1914	Lysander	16f	4:25	F. A. Clark
1915	Weldship	16f	4:25	E. M. Weld
1916	Weldship	16f	4:19	E. M. Weld
1917	Weldship	16f	4:16 4/5	E. M. Weld
1918	Bet	16f	4:16 2/5	W. R. Coe
1919	Elysian	16f	4:23 1/5	Mrs. F. A. Clark
1920	Flare	16f	4:22	Greentree Stable
1921	Sweepment	16f	4:22 1/5	Mrs. G. W. Loft
1922	Soumangha	16f	4:18	Greentree Stable
1923	Bullseye	16f	4:18 2/5	J. S. Cosden
1924	El Kantara	16f	4:12	J. E. Davis
1925	Away II	16f	4:22	Mr. Coates
1926	Lorenzo	16f	4:17 3/5	J. E. Widener
1927	Thorndale	16f	4:14 4/5	Sewickley Stable
1928	Rabel	16f	4:20	J. Livingston
1929	Coronation	16f	4:15 2/5	Greentree Stable
1930	Jolly Roger	16f	4:13 1/5	Greentree Stable
1931	Indigo	16f	4:18	J. E. Widener
1932	Barometer	16f	4:18 3/5	E. R. Bradley
1933	Cherry Brandy	16f	4:12 1/5	Greentree Stable

1934	Best Play	16f	4:11 1/5	M. Sanford
1935	Rhadamanthus	16f	4:15	G. Whitney
1936	Jungle King	16f	4:22 4/5	Greentree Stable
1937	Sailor Beware	16f	4:11 1/5	Greentree Stable
1938	Ossabaw	16f	4:13 4/5	T. Hitchcock
1939	Cottesmore	16f	4:12 2/5	T. Hitchcock
1940	Cottesmore	16f	4:16 4/5	G. H. Bostwick
1941	Bay Dean	16f	4:16	Mrs. A. White
1942	Elkridge	16f	4:19 3/5	K. Miller
1943	Elkridge	16f	3:52	K. Miller
1944	Ossabaw	16f	3:49	T. T. Mott
1945	Floating Isle	16f	3:45	T. T. Mott
1946	Elkridge	16f	4:15 4/5	K. Miller
1947	Great Flares	16f	4:16 2/5	Mrs. F. A. Clark
1948	Elkridge	16f	4:14 1/5	K. Miller
1949	Sun Bath	16f	4:12 1/5	R. W. Grant
1950	The Heir	16f	4:09 4/5	Mrs. C. Sullivan
1951	Cherwell	16f	4:48 4/5	Mrs. E. DuPont Weir
1952	Jam	16f	4:27 4/5	J. F. McHugh
1953	The Mast	16f	4:09 3/5	Mrs. E. DuPont Weir
1954	Escargto	16f	4:13	Mrs. C. E. Adams
1955	Rhythminhim	16f	4:18	Mrs. M. G. Walsh

SANFORD STAKES

1913	Little Nephew	6f	1:14 4/5	M. B. Gruber
1914	Regret	6f	1:13 2/5	H. P. Whitney
1915	Bulse	6f	1:16 4/5	J. W. Parrish
1916	Campfire	6f	1:13 2/5	R. T. Wilson

THE SARATOGA ASSOCIATION
FOR THE IMPROVEMENT OF THE BREED OF HORSES
6 AND 8 EAST 46TH STREET
NEW YORK

1917	Papp	6f	1:15 3/5	G. W. Loft
1918	Billy Kelly	6f	1:14 3/5	J. K. L. Ross
1919	Upset	6f	1:11 1/5	H. P. Whitney
1920	Pluribus	6f	1:15 1/5	T. W. O'Brien
1921	Sir Hugh	6f	1:13	J. N. Camden
1922	Bo McMillan	6f	1:18	T. J. Prendergast
1923	Parasol	6f	1:12 4/5	G. D. Widener
1924	Nicholas	6f	1:15 3/5	F. Farrell
1925	Canter	6f	1:12 3/5	J. E. Griffith
1926	Northland	6f	1:13	W. Salmon
1927	Nassak	6f	1:12 2/5	Rancocas Stable
1928	Chestnut Oak	6f	1:13	Oak Ridge Stable
1929	Hi Jack	6f	1:12	G. D. Widener
1930	Sun Meadow	6f	1:12 3/5	Mrs. K. E. Hitt
1931	Mad Pursuit	6f	1:12 1/5	W. Salmon
1932	Sun Archer	6f	1:12 4/5	W. S. Kilmer
1933	First Minstrel	6f	1:15	Greentree
1934	Psychic Bid	6f	1:12 1/5	Brookmeade Stable
1935	Crossbow II	6f	1:12 2/5	Calumet Farm
1936	Maedic	6f	1:13	Maemare Farm
1937	Spillway	6f	1:14	J. W. Brown
1938	Birch Road	6f	1:14 1/5	G. D. Widener
1939	Boy Angler	6f	1:12 1/5	Mr. French
1940	Good Turn	6f	1:13 1/5	A. G. Vanderbilt
1941	Devil Diver	6f	1:12 4/5	Greentree Stable
1942	Devil's Thumb	6f	1:12 4/5	W. E. Boeing
1943	Rodney Stone	6f	1:11 1/5	H. LaMontagne
1944	The Doge	6f	1:10 2/5	Pentagon Stable

1945	Pellicle	6f	1:10 4/5	H. P. Headley
1946	Donor	6f	1:11 3/5	D. Howe
1947	Inseparable	6f	1:11 4/5	Brookmeade Stable
1948	Slam Bang	6f	1:12	C. M. Kline
1949	Detective	6f	1:12 4/5	Mrs. A. Wichfield
1950	Big Stretch	6f	1:11 3/5	Greentree Stable
1951	Tom Fool	6f	1:12 3/5	Greentree Stable
1952	Bradley	6f	1:14 3/5	Mrs. C. O. Iselin
1953	Bobby Brocato	6f	1:13 1/5	J. W. Brown
1954	Brother Tex	6f	1:12 4/5	W. Stephens
1955	Head Man	6f	1:11 4/5	C. V. Whitney

NOTE: Run as the Sanford Memorial Stakes prior to 1927. Ariel Toy finished first in 1938, but was disqualified

SARANAC HANDICAP

1901	Dublin	9f	1:52 3/5	Goughacres Stable
1902	Hermis	9f	1:51 2/5	L. V. Bell
1903	Molly Brant	9f	1:55 1/5	J. Sanford
1904	Dolly Spanker	9f	1:55 1/5	R. T. Wilson
1905	Dandelion	9f	1:53 4/5	F. Hitchcock
1906	Gallavant	9f	1:56 3/5	R. T. Wilson
1907	Vails	9f	1:53 2/5	J. Sanford
1908	Golconda	9f	1:57 3/5	E. Marryatt
1909	Field Mouse	8f	1:37 3/5	A. Belmont
1910	Martinez	9f	1:52 1/5	H. LaMontagne
1913	Ten Point	8f	1:39	A. L. Aste

THE SARATOGA ASSOCIATION
FOR THE IMPROVEMENT OF THE BREED OF HORSES
6 AND 8 EAST 46TH STREET
NEW YORK

1914	Stromboli	8f	1:38 3/5	A. Belmont
1915	Regret	8f	1:42	L. S. Thompson
1916	Dodge	8f	1:38	J. S. Ward
1917	Midway	8f	1:39 2/5	J. W. Parrish
1918	Motor Cop	8f	1:36 4/5	A. K. Macomber
1919	Purchase	8f	1:42 1/5	S. C. Hildreth
1920	Dinna Care	8f	1:38 3/5	Glen Riddle Farm
1921	Crocus	8f	1:37 4/5	H. P. Whitney
1922	Little Chief	8f	1:37 4/5	Rancocas Stable
1923	Cherry Pie	8f	1:38	Greentree Stable
1924	Sarazen	8f	1:37 3/5	Fair Stable
1925	Peanuts	8f	1:39	R. L. Gerry
1926	Mars	8f	1:39	W. M. Jeffords
1927	Osmand	8f	1:39 3/5	J. E. Widener
1928	Sun Edwin	8f	1:41 3/5	Arden Farms
1929	Hard Tack	8f	1:37 2/5	Wheatley Stable
1930	Whichone	8f	1:37	H. P. Whitney
1931	Danour	8f	1:40 1/5	D. D. Moore
1932	Morfair	8f	1:41 2/5	J. P. Smith
1933	War Glory	8f	1:38 3/5	Glen Riddle Farm
1934	Kievex	8f	1:37 1/5	W. Graham
1935	Good Gamble	8f	1:38 2/5	A. G. Vanderbilt
1936	Sun Teddy	8f	1:40 1/5	Calumet Farm
1937	Burning Star	8f	1:39 2/5	Shandon Farm
1938	Thanksgiving	8f	1:38 4/5	Mrs. P. Corning
1939	Heather Broom	8f	1:38 4/5	J. H. Whitney
1940	Parasang	8f	1:38 1/5	C. V. Whitney
1941	Whirlaway	8f	1:38	Calumet Farm

1942	Bless Me	8f	1:37 1/5	E. R. Bradley
1943	Water Pearl	8f	1:36 3/5	Hudson Valley Stable
1944	Hoodoo	8.5f	1:44	C. V. Whitney
1945	Polynesian	6f	1:10 2/5	Mrs. P. A. B. Widener
1946	Aladear	8f	1:38 3/5	A. C. Ernst
1948	Mount Marcy	8.5f	1:44 4/5	C. V. Whitney
1949	Sun Bahram	8.5f	1:45	Mrs. E. H. Ellison Jr.
1950	Sunglow	8.5f	1:43 3/5	Brookmeade Stable
1951	Bold	8.5f	1:43 3/5	Brookmeade Stable
1952	Golden Gloves	8.5f	1:45 2/5	Belair Stud
1953	First Aid	8.5f	1:43 4/5	Brookmeade Stable
1954	Full Flight	8.5f	1:44 4/5	Wheatley Stable
1955	Saratoga	8.5f	1:44	Montpelier Stable

NOTE: Not run in 1947, and run at Jamaica 1948-1955.

SARATOGA CUP

1901	Blues	13f	2:52 2/5	F. Farrell
1902	Advance Guard	14f	3:01 4/5	Carruthers & Shields
1903	Africander	14f	2:58	Hampton Stable
1904	Beldame	14f	3:03 4/5	N. Bennington
1905	Caughnawaga	14f	3:00 4/5	J. Sanford
1906	Go Between	14f	3:05 2/5	E. R. Thomas
1907	Running Water	14f	3:06 1/5	Newcastle Stable
1909	Olambala	14f	2:58	Montpelier Stable
1910	Countless	14f	2:58 3/5	J. G. Greener
1913	Sam Jackson	14f	3:08 2/5	V. M. McGinnes

THE SARATOGA ASSOCIATION
FOR THE IMPROVEMENT OF THE BREED OF HORSES
6 AND 8 EAST 46TH STREET
NEW YORK

1914	Star Gaze	14f	3:10	H. C. Pratt
1915	Roamer	14f	3:01 4/5	A. Miller
1916	Friar Rock	14f	3:03	A. Belmont
1917	Omar Khayyam	14f	3:07 4/5	W. Viau
1918	Johren	14f	3:02 1/5	H. P. Whitney
1919	Exterminator	14f	2:58	W. S. Kilmer
1920	Exterminator	14f	2:56 2/5	W. S. Kilmer
1921	Exterminator	14f	3:04 3/5	W. S. Kilmer
1922	Exterminator	14f	3:00 2/5	W. S. Kilmer
1923	My Own	14f	2:57 1/5	Salubria Stable
1924	Mr. Mutt	14f	3:00 4/5	H.C. Fisher
1925	Mad Play	14f	2:59 2/5	Rancocas Stable
1926	Espino	14f	3:00 2/5	W. Ziegler Jr.
1927	Chance Play	14f	3:03 3/5	Arden Farm
1928	Reigh Count	14f	2:55	Mrs. J. D. Hertz
1929	Diavaolo	14f	2:58	Wheatley Stable
1930	Gallant Fox	14f	2:56	Belair Stud
1931	Twenty Grand	14f	3:01 1/5	Greentree Stable
1932	War Hero	14f	2:59 1/5	Glen Riddle Farm
1933	Equipoise	14f	3:00	C. V. Whitney
1934	Dark Secret	14f	2:59 1/5	Wheatley Stable
1935	Count Arthur	14f	2:58 2/5	Mrs. J. D. Hertz
1936	Granville	14f	3:00 4/5	Belair Stud
1937	Count Arthur	14f	3:02 1/5	Mrs. J. D. Hertz
1938	War Admiral	14f	2:55 4/5	Glen Riddle Farm
1939	Isolator	14f	2:56 1/5	Belair Stud
1940	Isolator	14f	3:02	Belair Stud
1941	Dorimar	14f	2:58 2/5	Woodvale Farm

THE SARATOGA ASSOCIATION
FOR THE IMPROVEMENT OF THE BREED OF HORSES
6 AND 8 EAST 46TH STREET
NEW YORK

1942	Bolingbroke	14f	2:58 1/5	T. B. Martin
1943	Princequillo	14f	2:56 3/5	Boone Hill Stable
1944	Bolingbroke	14f	2:57 3/5	T. B. Martin
1945	Stymie	14f	2:58	Mrs. E. D. Jacobs
1946	Stymie	14f	3:07 2/5	Mrs. E. D. Jacobs
1947	Talon	14f	2:58 2/5	R. N. Ryan
1948	Snow Goose	14f	2:57 4/5	W. M. Jeffords
1949	Doubtless II	14f	2:57 2/5	Greentree Stable
1950	Cochise	14f	2:57 3/5	Brandywine Stable
1951	Busanda	14f	2:59	O. Phipps
1952	Busanda	14f	2:59 4/5	O. Phipps
1953	Alerted	14f	3:01 1/5	Hampton Stable
1954	Great Captain	14f	3:02 2/5	O. Phipps
1955	Chevation	14f	3:02 3/5	Foxcatcher Farm

NOTE: Not run in 1908. In 1940, Isolator and Fenelon were coupled as an entry and there was no betting, the race being a walkover. The race was also a walkover for Stymie in 1946.

SARATOGA HANDICAP

1901	Rockton	9f	1:53 1/5	W.H. Sealey
1902	Francesco	9.5f	1:59	C. F. Dwyer
1903	Water Boy	10f	2:05 3/5	J. B. Haggin
1904	Lord of the Vale	10f	2:05	A. Belmont
1905	Caughnawaga	10f	2:07	J. Sanford
1906	Dandelion	10f	2:04 3/5	J. R. Keene
1907	McCarter	10f	2:05 3/5	Newcastle Stable

THE SARATOGA ASSOCIATION
FOR THE IMPROVEMENT OF THE BREED OF HORSES
6 AND 8 EAST 46TH STREET
NEW YORK

1908	Montfort	10f	2:05 4/5	Montpelier Stable
1909	Affliction	10f	2:05	J. R. Keene
1910	Olambala	10f	2:08 3/5	R. T. Wilson
1913	Cock o' the Walk	10f	2:06	F. Johnson
1914	Borrow	10f	2:05 2/5	H. P. Whitney
1915	Roamer	10f	2:04 2/5	A. Miller
1916	Stromboli	10f	2:05 1/5	A. Belmont
1917	Roamer	10f	2:06 1/5	A. Miller
1918	Roamer	10f	2:02 1/5	A. Miller
1919	Purchase	10f	2:02 2/5	S. C. Hildreth
1920	Sir Barton	10f	2:01 4/5	J. K. L. Ross
1921	Yellow Hand	10f	2:03 4/5	C. A. Stoneham
1922	Grey Lag	10f	2:03 1/5	Rancocas Stable
1923	Prince James	10f	2:09 2/5	C. H. Thierot
1924	My Own	10f	2:05 3/5	Salubria Stable
1925	Valador	10f	2:05 3/5	W. Martin
1926	Princess Doreen	10f	2:08 2/5	Audley Farm
1927	Mars	10f	2:07 3/5	W. M. Jeffords
1928	Chance Shot	10f	2:06	J. E. Widener
1929	Diavolo	10f	2:03 3/5	Wheatley Stable
1930	Marine	10f	2:04 1/5	Mount Royal Stable
1931	St. Brideaux	10f	2:04	Mrs. P. Whitney
1932	Faireno	10f	2:04 3/5	Belair Stud
1933	Caesars Ghost	10f	2:07 1/5	Brookmeade Stable
1934	Watch Him	10f	2:06 3/5	Mrs. J. D. Hertz
1935	Vicar	10f	2:04 4/5	Belair Stud
1936	Discovery	10f	2:05	A. G. Vanderbilt
1937	Esposa	10f	2:08 2/5	Wm. Ziegler Jr.

THE SARATOGA ASSOCIATION
FOR THE IMPROVEMENT OF THE BREED OF HORSES
6 AND 8 EAST 46TH STREET
NEW YORK

1938	War Admiral	10f	2:06	Glen Riddle Farm
1939	Eight Thirty	10f	2:03 3/5	G. D. Widener
1940	Sickle T	10f	2:03	Mrs. B. F. Whitaker
1941	Haltal	10f	2:05 4/5	Woodvale Farm
1942	Can't Wait	10f	2:05	M. Selznick
1943	Princequillo	10f	2:01 4/5	Boone Hill Stable
1944	Paperboy	10f	2:02 1/5	W-L Ranch
1945	Olympic Zenith	10f	2:02 4/5	W. Helis
1946	Lucky Draw	10f	2:01 3/5	G. D. Widener
1947	Rico Monte	10f	2:03 2/5	A. Hanger
1948	Loyal Legion	10f	2:03 1/5	W. M. Jeffords
1949	Donor	10f	2:04	Mrs. D. Howe
1950	Better Self	10f	2:05 3/5	King Ranch
1951	Lone Eagle	10f	2:04	G. Ring
1952	One Hitter	10f	2:05	Greentree Stable
1953	Alerted	10f	2:05 3/5	Hampton Stable
1954	Cold Command	10f	2:05 4/5	C. V. Whitney
1955	Social Outcast	10f	2:04 2/5	A. G. Vanderbilt

SARATOGA SPECIAL

1901	Goldsmith	5.5f	1:08 1/5	W. C. Whitney
1902	Irish Lad	5.5f	1:08 1/5	Whitney & Duryea
1903	Aristocracy	5.5f	1:11 4/5	J. E. Madden
1904	Sysonby	5.5f	1:07	J. R. Keene
1905	Mohawk II	5.5f	1:07	J. Sanford
1906	Salvidere	6f	1:12 2/5	T. Hitchcock
1907	Colin	6f	1:12	J. R. Keene

Year	Horse	Dist	Time	Owner
1908	Sir Martin	6f	1:18 4/5	J. E. Madden
1909	Waldo	6f	1:15 4/5	C. L. Harrison
1910	Novelty	6f	1:14 2/5	S. C. Hildreth
1913	Roamer	6f	1:13	A. Miller
1914	Regret	6f	1:11 3/5	H. P. Whitney
1915	Dominant	6f	1:16	L. S. Thompson
1916	Campfire	6f	1:13 1/5	R. T. Wilson
1917	Sun Briar	6f	1:15	W. S. Kilmer
1918	Hannibal	6f	1:16 1/5	R. T. Wilson
1919	Golden Broom	6f	1:12 4/5	Mrs. W. M. Jeffords
1920	Tryster	6f	1:12 3/5	H. P. Whitney
1921	Morvich	6f	1:12 1/5	B. Block
1922	Goshawk	6f	1:12 1/5	H. P. Whitney
1923	St. James	6f	1:11 3/5	G. D. Widener
1924	Sunnyman	6f	1:12 3/5	W. S. Kilmer
1925	Haste	6f	1:12 2/5	J. E. Widener
1926	Chance Shot	6f	1:13	J. E. Widener
1927	Ariel	6f	1:12 3/5	Rancocas Stable
1928	Blue Larkspur	6f	1:13 3/5	Idle Hour Farm
1929	Whichone	6f	1:13 4/5	H. P. Whitney
1930	Jamestown	6f	1:11 2/5	G. D. Widener
1931	Top Flight	6f	1:12	C. V. Whitney
1932	Happy Gal	6f	1:13	Belair Stud
1933	Wise Daughter	6f	1:12 3/5	F. A. Burton
1934	Boxthorn	6f	1:12 1/5	E. R. Bradley
1935	Red Rain	6f	1:13	C. V. Whitney
	Coldstream (dh)			E. D. Shaffer
1936	Forty Winks	6f	1:13 4/5	Greentree Stable

THE SARATOGA ASSOCIATION
FOR THE IMPROVEMENT OF THE BREED OF HORSES
6 AND 8 EAST 46TH STREET
NEW YORK

1937	Pumpkin	6f	1:12 3/5	J. H. Whitney
1938	El Chico	6f	1:10 2/5	W. Ziegler Jr.
1939	Bimelech	6f	1:10 4/5	E. R. Bradley
1940	Whirlaway	6f	1:11 1/5	Calumet Farm
1941	Ampitheatre	6f	1:11 3/5	Manhasset Stable
1942	Halberd	6f	1:13	Mrs. W. M. Jeffords
1943	Cocopet	6f	1:10 3/5	Lazy F Ranch
1944	Pavot	6f	1:09 3/5	W. M. Jeffords
1945	Mist O' Gold	6f	1:10 3/5	Vera S. Bragg
1946	Grand Admiral	6f	1:13 2/5	Brookmeade Stable
1947	Better Self	6f	1:12 4/5	King Ranch
1948	Blue Peter	6f	1:13	J. M. Roebling
1949	More Sun	6f	1:13 4/5	Brookmeade Stable
1950	Battlefield	6f	1:11 1/5	G. D. Widener
1951	Cousin	6f	1:12	A. G. Vanderbilt
1952	Native Dancer	6f	1:13 1/5	A. G. Vanderbilt
1953	Turn-To	6f	1:12 4/5	Llangollen Farm
1954	Royal Coinage	6f	1:12 1/5	Clearwater St.
1955	Polly's Jet	6f	1:11 2/5	Barclay Stable

NOTE: Red Rain, owned by C. V. Whitney, and Coldstream, owned by E. D. Shaffer, finished in a deadheat in the 1935 Saratoga Special. After the race, the owners held a coin toss in front of the stands to determine who should take home the trophy, with Mr. Shaffer the winner. Saratoga Association president Richard T. Wilson asked about the coin toss, and upon learning of it decided to award a trophy to each owner. This brought applause from the 25,000 fans in attendance. As reported by the *New York Times* of Aug. 11, 1935. Porterhouse finished first in 1953, but was disqualified.

THE SARATOGA ASSOCIATION
FOR THE IMPROVEMENT OF THE BREED OF HORSES
6 AND 8 EAST 46TH STREET
NEW YORK

SARATOGA STEEPLECHASE

1906	Herculoid	16f	4:19	C. Pfizer
1907	El Cuchillo	16f	4:16	J. E. Widener
1908	Jimmy Lane	16f	4:25 2/5	G. Tompkins
1909	Ballacalla	16f	4:20 4/5	R. Neville
1910	Hylda	20f	5:24	F. A. Clark
1913	Wickson	20f	5:24	L. A. Ekers
1914	Lysander	20f	5:23	F. A. Clark
1915	Weldship	20f	5:23	E. M. Weld
1916	Pebeto	20f	5:18	H. W. Sage
1917	St. Charlcote	20f	5:22 2/5	E. M. Weld
1918	St. Charlcote	20f	5:18 3/5	E. M. Weld
1919	Hibler	20f	5:23	Mrs. F. A. Clark
1920	Minata	20f	5:27 2/5	Mrs. F. A. Clark
1921	Robert Oliver	20f	5:17 3/5	J. Lumsden
1922	Houdini	20f	5:24	J. E. Widener
1923	Dan IV	20f	5:13 2/5	J. S. Cosden
1924	Dunks Green	20f	5:23	W. J. Salmon
1925	Carabinier	20f	5:17	J. F. Byers
1926	Erne II	20f	5:11 3/5	Greentree Stable
1927	Lorenzo	20f	5:22	J. E. Widener
1928	Thracian	20f	5:14 1/5	Sanford Stud
1929	Huffy	20f	5:08	W. J. Salmon
1930	Devilkin	20f	5:10	J. Simpson
1931	Beacon Hill	20f	5:24	C. V. Whitney
1932	Barometer	20f	5:14 2/5	E. R. Bradley

1933	Blot	20f	5:06 2/5	G. Whitney
1934	Irish Bullet	20f	5:09 4/5	F. A. Clark
1935	Jungle King	20f	5:08 4/5	Greentree Stable
1936	Rioter	20f	5:24 2/5	T. Hitchcock
1937	Galsac	20f	5:10 2/5	Greentree Stable
1938	Ossabaw	20f	5:06 2/5	T. Hitchcock
1939	Cottesmore	20f	6:18	T. Hitchcock
1940	Dolly's Love	20f	5:19	E. B. Schley
1941	Invader	20f	5:09	Mrs. F. A. Clark
1942	Iron Shot	20f	5:11 4/5	Miss E. Widener
1943	Iron Shot	20f	4:47	Miss E. Widener
1944	Elkridge	20f	4:49 1/5	K. Miller
1945	Rouge Dragon	20f	4:51	M. A. Cushman
1946	Replica II	20f	5:08 2/5	R. K. Mellon
1947	Floating Isle	20f	5:20	T. T. Mott
1948	Tourist List	20f	5:11	L. Watkins
1949	Sun Bath	20f	5:06 3/5	R. W. Grant
1950	Elkridge	20f	5:08 2/5	K. Miller
1951	Hampton Roads	20f	5:05 3/5	Montpelier Stable
1952	Banner Waves	20f	5:06 4/5	R. McKinney
1953	Sun Shower	20f	5:06 3/5	Mrs. V. G. Cardy
1954	King Commander	20f	5:00 2/5	L. R. Troiano
1955	Shipboard	20f	5:06 3/5	Montpelier Stable

SCHUYLERVILLE STAKES

| 1918 | Tuscaloosa | 5.5f | 1:04 3/5 | J. Sanford |
| 1919 | Homely | 5.5f | 1:06 2/5 | L. Waterbury |

1920	Careful	5.5f	1:05 3/5	W. J. Salmon
1921	Miss Joy	5.5f	1:05 3/5	M. Jones
1922	Edict	5.5f	1:08 4/5	Rancocas Stable
1923	Befuddle	5.5f	1:05 4/5	Idle Hour Stable
1924	Royalite	5.5f	1:08 2/5	Rancocas Stable
1925	Taps	5.5f	1:07	Glen Riddle Farm
1926	Aromagne	5.5f	1:07 2/5	W. S. Kilmer
1927	Pennant Queen	5.5f	1:07	Mrs. L. Viau
1928	Atlantis	5.5f	1:07 2/5	G. D. Widener
1929	Flying Gal	5.5f	1:05 2/5	Belair Stud
1930	Panasette	5.5f	1:06	H. P. Whitney
1931	Polonaise	5.5f	1:08	W. R. Coe
1932	Volette	5.5f	1:07 3/5	C. V. Whitney
1933	Slapdash	5.5f	1:06	Wheatley Stable
1934	Uppermost	5.5f	1:05 3/5	M. L. Schwartz
1935	Parade Girl	5.5f	1:06 1/5	A. G. Vanderbilt
1936	Maecloud	5.5f	1:07 3/5	Maemare Farm
1937	Creole Maid	5.5f	1:05 4/5	Mrs. W. M. Jeffords
1938	Soldierette	5.5f	1:05 3/5	W. J. Hirsch
1939	Teacher	5.5f	1:05 3/5	Brookmeade Stable
1940	Nasca	5.5f	1:05 1/5	B. Long
1941	Romp Home	5.5f	1:06 2/5	W. Ziegler Jr.
1942	Brittany	5.5f	1:06 4/5	J. M. Roebling
1943	Boojiana	5.5f	1:04 2/5	C. V. Whitney
1944	Ace Card	5.5f	1:04 3/5	Mrs. W. M. Jeffords
1945	Red Shoes	5.5f	1:04 3/5	H. E. Jackson
1946	Bright Song	5.5f	1:07 2/5	C. V. Whitney
1947	Spats	5.5f	1:04 4/5	E. P. Taylor

1948	Gaffery	5.5f	1:07	Foxcatcher Farms
1949	Striking	5.5f	1:05 2/5	O. Phipps
1950	Atalanta	5.5f	1:06	Brookmeade Stable
1951	Rose Jet	5.5f	1:06 1/5	Main Chance Farm
1952	Grecian Queen	5.5f	1:07 2/5	Mrs. B. F. Whitaker
1953	Evening Out	5.5f	1:05 2/5	G. D. Widener
1954	Two Stars	5.5f	1:05 4/5	H. A. Flanagan
1955	Dark Charger	5.5f	1:05 3/5	H. W. Kellogg

NOTE: There was a Schuylerville Selling Handicap run in 1916 for 3-year-olds, and a Schuylerville Handicap for older horses run in 1917. Run at Jamaica in 1952.

SHILLELAH STEEPLECHASE

1902	Clasher	20f	5:10 3/5	H. S. Page
1903	Lavator	20f	5:04	J. W. Colt
1904	Foxhunter	20f	5:01	T. Hitchcock
1905	Gatebell	20f	5:29	J. E. Widener
1906	Grandpa	20f	5:19	W. C. Hayes
1907	McKittredge	20f	5:20	F. A. Clark
1908	Bayonet	20f	5:31	W. Walker
1909	Byzantine	20f	5:22	N. Ray
1910	Aunt Jule	16f	4:21	Lexington Stable
1913	Shannon River	20f	5:36 2/5	R. Parr
1914	El Bart	20f	5:20	J. E. Widener
1915	El Bart	20f	5:27	J. E. Widener
1916	Weldship	16f	4:19	E. M. Weld

1917	Al Reeves	16f	4:23	Greentree Stable
1918	The Brook	16f	4:23 4/5	J. E. Griffith
1919	Doublet	16f	4:20	J. E. Widener
1920	Flare	16f	4:27 2/5	E. C. Griffith
1921	Minata	16f	4:23	Mrs. F. A. Clark
1922	Minata	16f	4:23	Mrs. F. A. Clark
1923	Bullseye	16f	4:23 2/5	J. S. Gosden
1924	Autumn Bells	16f	4:17	J. B. Smith
1925	Upsal	16f	4:22	B. Warren
1926	Erne II	16f	4:17	Greentree Stable
1927	Brantome	16f	4:26 2/5	Greentree Stable
1928	Thracian	16f	4:24 4/5	Sanford Stud
1929	Coronation	16f	4:17	Mrs. H. P. Whitney
1930	Wayfare	16f	4:18	Rolling Plains St.
1931	Cawvoge	16f	4:16	Mrs. P. Whitney
1932	Dark Magne	16f	4:11 4/5	S. Sanford
1933	Lord Johnson	16f	4:25 2/5	Mrs. M.L. Schwartz
1934	Irish Bullet	16f	4:12 3/5	F. A. Clark
1935	Golden Meadow	16f	4:08 2/5	Sanford Stud
1936	Rioter	16f	4:09	T. Hitchcock
1937	National Anthem	16f	4:14	Brookmeade Stable
1938	National Anthem	16f	4:18 1/5	Brookmeade Stable
1939	Saluda	16f	4:09 1/5	T. Hitchcock
1940	Ossabaw	16f	4:18 1/5	L. B. Mayer
1941	Speculate	16f	4:13 2/5	B. Sharp
1942	Lovely Night	16f	4:14	Mrs. F. A. Clark
1943	Delhi Dan	16f	3:48 2/5	Brookmeade Stable
1944	Elkridge	16f	3:48	K. Miller

1945	Raylwyn	16f	3:49 1/5	Mrs. F. A. Clark
1946	Tetrol	16f	4:15	R. A. Firestone
1947	Tourist List	16f	4:14	L. Watkins
1948	Elkridge	16f	4:14 1/5	K. Miller
1949	Galactic	16f	4:20	Mrs. E. D. Weir
1950	Oedipus	16f	4:10 2/5	Mrs. O. Phipps
1951	Banner Waves	16f	4:16 4/5	R. McKinney
1952	Oedipus	16f	4:11	Mrs. O. Phipps
1953	Sun Shower	16f	4:10	Mrs. V. G. Cardy
1954	Shipboard	16f	4:17 2/5	Montpelier Stable
1955	Fulton	16f	4:07 4/5	Sanford Stud

SPINAWAY STAKES

1901	Rossignol	5.5f	1:10 2/5	T. Hitchcock
1902	Duster	5.5f	1:10 4/5	J. & F. Keene
1903	Raglan	5.5f	1:12 2/5	F. Gebhard
1904	Tanya	5.5f	1:07 3/5	H. B. Duryea
1905	Edna Jackson	5.5f	1:08 4/5	P. McCarren
1906	Court Dress	5.5f	1:07	J. R. Keene
1907	Julia Powell	5.5f	1:06 4/5	W.B. Jennings
1908	Maskette	5.5f	1:05 4/5	J. R. Keene
1909	Ocean Bound	5.5f	1:06 3/5	W. Clay
1910	Bashi	5.5f	1:06 4/5	Newcastle Stable
1913	Casuarina	5.5f	1:07	J. N. Camden
1914	Lady Barbary	5.5f	1:06	R. F. Carman
1915	Jacoby	5.5f	1:11	J. O. Keene
1916	Yankee Witch	5.5f	1:07 2/5	Glen Riddle Farm

THE SARATOGA ASSOCIATION
FOR THE IMPROVEMENT OF THE BREED OF HORSES
6 AND 8 EAST 46TH STREET
NEW YORK

1917	Olive Wood	5.5f	1:07 2/5	T. C. McDowell
1918	Passing Shower	5.5f	1:05 3/5	J. H. Rosseter
1919	Constancy	5.5f	1:05 3/5	J. K. L. Ross
1920	Prudery	5.5f	1:05	H. P. Whitney
1921	Miss Joy	5.5f	1:05 1/5	M. Jones
1922	Edict	5.5f	1:09	Rancocas Stable
1923	Anna Marrone II	6f	1:12 3/5	Marrone Stable
1924	Blue Warbler	6f	1:12	Idle Hour Farm
1925	Cinema	6f	1:15 2/5	S. Ross
1926	Bonnie Pennant	6f	1:14 2/5	H. P. Whitney
1927	Twitter	6f	1:12	H. P. Whitney
1928	Atlantis	6f	1:15	G. D. Widener
1929	Goose Egg	6f	1:12 1/5	Greentree Stable
1930	Risque	6f	1:16 3/5	Mr. & Mrs. J.D. Hertz
1931	Top Flight	6f	1:12 2/5	C. V. Whitney
1932	Easy Day	6f	1:13 2/5	Greentree Stable
1933	Contessa	6f	1:15	Mrs. J. D. Hertz
1934	Vicaress	6f	1:12 4/5	Belair Stud
1935	Forever Yours	6f	1:12 4/5	Milky Way Farm
1936	Maecloud	6f	1:14 1/5	Maemare Farm
1937	Merry Lassie	6f	1:12 1/5	Wheatley Stable
1938	Dinner Date	6f	1:13	Milky Way Farm
1939	Now What	6f	1:13 1/5	A. G. Vanderbilt
1940	Nasca	6f	1:12	B. Long
1941	Mar-Kell	6f	1:13 3/5	Calumet Farm
1942	Our Page	6f	1:12 3/5	Woodvale Farm
1943	Bee Mac	6f	1:12 2/5	B. MacGuire
1944	Price Level	6F	1:12 1/5	C. Oglebay

1945	Sopranist	6f	1:09 1/5	W. H. Laboyteaux
1946	Pipette	6f	1:11	W. H. Laboyteaux
1947	Bellesoeur	6f	1:11 3/5	Mrs. L. Lawrence
1948	Myrtle Charm	6f	1:11 3/5	Maine Chance Farm
1949	Sunday Evening	6f	1:11 2/5	Greentree Stable
1950	Atalanta	6f	1:13	Brookmeade Stable
1951	Blue Case	6f	1:13 1/5	J. M. Roebling
1952	Flirtatious	6f	1:13 1/5	O. Phipps
1953	Evening Out	6f	1:13 3/5	G. D. Widener
1954	Gandharva	6f	1:12 4/5	Brookmeade Stable
1955	Register	6f	1:13 2/5	Greentree Stable

NOTE: Inaugurated in 1881, the Spinaway is the oldest stakes race for two-year-old fillies in the United States.

TEST STAKES

1922	Emotion	10f	2:11 1/5	R. L. Gerry
1926	Ruthenia	7f	1:25 2/5	J. E. Widener
1927	Black Curl	7f	1:26 3/5	Rancocas Stable
1928	Nixie	7f	1:25 4/5	Wheatley Stable
1929	Dinah Did Upset	7f	1:24 4/5	S. W. Labrot
1930	Conclave	7f	1:24 1/5	W. R. Coe
1931	Buckup	7f	1:25 4/5	J. E. Widener
1932	Suntica	7f	1:26	W. S. Kilmer
1933	Speed Boat	7f	1:24 1/5	Glen Riddle Farm
1934	Bazaar	7f	1:24 3/5	E. R. Bradley
1935	Good Gamble	7f	1:24 4/5	A. G. Vanderbilt

1936	Fair Stein	7f	1:24 4/5	H. Phillips
1937	Evening Tide	7f	1:26	E. D. Shaffer
1938	Black Wave	7f	1:25 4/5	Nydrie Stud
1939	Redlin	7f	1:24	W. H. Lipscomb
1940	Piquet	7f	1:24 2/5	Greentree Stable
1941	Imperatrice	7f	1:25 1/5	W. H. Laboyteaux
1942	Vagrancy	7f	1:26	Belair Stud
1943	Stefanita	7f	1:25 1/5	G. D. Widener
1944	Whirlabout	7f	1:24 4/5	L. B. Mayer
1945	Safeguard	7f	1:24 1/5	Brookmeade Stable
1946	Red Shoes	7f	1:23 2/5	H. E. Jackson
1947	Miss Disco	7f	1:24 2/5	S. S. Schupper
1948	Alablue	7f	1:25 4/5	J. H. Skirvin
1949	Lady Dorimar	7f	1:25 1/5	Woodvale Farm
1950	Honey's Gal	7f	1:24 2/5	F. E. Dixon Jr.
1951	Vulcania	7f	1:26	Belair Stud
1952	Gay Grecque	7f	1:26 4/5	Mrs. S.G. Zauderer
1953	Canadiana	7f	1:25 3/5	E. P. Taylor
1954	Dispute	7f	1:25 1/5	C. V. Whitney
1955	Blue Banner	7f	1:24 3/5	Rokeby Stable

TRAVERS STAKES

1901	Blues	9f	1:56 3/5	Fleischmann's Sons
1902	Hermis	9f	1:54 4/5	H. M. Zeigler
1903	Ada Nay	9f	1:57	J. B. Haggin
1904	Broomstick	10f	2:06 4/5	S. S. Brown
1905	Dandelion	10f	2:08	F. Hitchcock

1906	Gallavant	10f	2:08 1/5	R. T. Wilson
1907	Frank Gill	10f	2:07	J. McGinnis
1908	Dorante	10f	2:09 3/5	F. A. Forsythe
1909	Hilarious	10f	2:06	J. R. Keene
1910	Dalmation	10f	2:10	S. C. Hildreth
1913	Rock View	10f	2:06 3/5	A. Belmont
1914	Roamer	10f	2:04	A. Miller
1915	Lady Rotha	10f	2:11 2/5	E. B. Cassatt
1916	Spur	10f	2:05	J. Butler
1917	Omar Khayyam	10f	2:08 4/5	W. Viau
1918	Sun Briar	10f	2:03 1/5	W. S. Kilmer
1919	Hannibal	10f	2:02 4/5	R. T. Wilson
1920	Man o' War	10f	2:01 4/5	Glen Riddle Farm
1921	Sporting Blood	10f	2:05 4/5	Redstone Stable
1922	Little Chief	10f	2:13 2/5	Rancocas Stable
1923	Wilderness	10f	2:04	R. T. Wilson
1924	Sun Flag	10f	2:04 2/5	G. A. Cochran
1925	Dangerous	10f	2:10 4/5	G. A. Cochran
1926	Mars	10f	2:04 3/5	W. M. Jeffords
1927	Brown Bud	10f	2:05 3/5	F. Johnson
1928	Petee-Wrack	10f	2:08	J. R. Macomber
1929	Beacon Hill	10f	2:04 1/5	H. P. Whitney
1930	Jim Dandy	10f	2:08	C. Earl
1931	Twenty Grand	10f	2:04 3/5	Greentree Stable
1932	War Hero	10f	2:05 4/5	Glen Riddle Farm
1933	Inlander	10f	2:08	Brookmeade Stable
1934	Observant	10f	2:05 3/5	M. L. Schwartz
1935	Gold Foam	10f	2:04 3/5	Starmount Stable

1936	Granville	10f	2:05 4/5	Belair Stud
1937	Burning Star	10f	2:04 4/5	Shandon Farm
1938	Thanksgiving	10f	2:03 3/5	Mrs. P. Corning
1939	Eight Thirty	10f	2:06 3/5	G. D. Widener
1940	Fenelon	10f	2:04 2/5	Belair Stud
1941	Whirlaway	10f	2:05 4/5	Calumet Farm
1942	Shut Out	10f	2:04 2/5	Greentree Stable
1943	Eurasian	10f	2:03 4/5	Mill River Stable
1944	By Jiminy	10f	2:03 2/5	A. P. Parker
1945	Adonis	10f	2:02 4/5	W. Helis
1946	Natchez	10f	2:08	Mrs. W. M. Jeffords
1947	Young Peter	10f	2:06 1/5	Mrs. R. L. Gerry
1948	Ace Admiral	10f	2:05	Maine Chance Farm
1949	Arise	10f	2:06 1/5	W. J. & H. Addison
1950	Lights Up	10f	2:03	G. D. Widener
1951	Battlefield	10f	2:06 1/5	G. D. Widener
1952	One Count	10f	2:07 2/5	Mrs. W. M. Jeffords
1953	Native Dancer	10f	2:05 3/5	A. G. Vanderbilt
1954	Fisherman	10f	2:06	C. V. Whitney
1955	Thinking Cap	10f	2:06 2/5	Christiana Stable

NOTE: The Travers, first run in 1864, is the oldest stakes race for three-year-olds in the United States. It was called the Travers Midsummer Derby from 1927 through 1932.

TROY STAKES

| 1901 | Five Nations | 5.5f | 1:07 3/5 | F. Farrell |

THE SARATOGA ASSOCIATION
FOR THE IMPROVEMENT OF THE BREED OF HORSES
6 AND 8 EAST 46TH STREET
NEW YORK

1902	Plater	5.5f	1:06 3/5	A. L. Aste
1903	Divination	5.5f	1:07 2/5	F. Regan
1904	Gold Ten	5.5f	1:07 4/5	W. Lakeland
1905	Rustling Silk	5.5f	1:07 1/5	M. Tichenor
1906	Loring	5.5f	1:06 2/5	F. Brown
1907	Frizette	5.5f	1:06 3/5	J. R. Keene
1908	Obdurate	5.5f	1:10 2/5	E. H. Hanna
1909	Mexoana	5.5f	1:07 4/5	Montpelier Stable
1910	Danger Mark	5.5f	1:07 1/5	Newcastle Stable
1913	Superintendent	5.5f	1:07 3/5	F. Mannix
1914	Headmast	5.5f	1:08 2/5	J. Fitzsimmons
1915	Success	5.5f	1:12 2/5	J. Fitzsimmons
1916	Katenka	5.5f	1:08	J. O. Keene
1917	Jack Hare Jr.	5.5f	1:07	W. E. Applegate
1918	Questionnaire	5.5f	1:05 4/5	E. Arlington
1919	His Choice	5.5f	1:08	J. K. L. Ross
1920	Tody	5.5f	1:05 3/5	W. P. Burch
1921	Modo	5.5f	1:05 4/5	Modo Stable
1922	Edict	5.5f	1:06	Rancocas Stable
1923	Rival	5.5f	1:07 3/5	Rancocas Stable
1924	Pedagogue	5.5f	1:06 3/5	Rancocas Stable
1925	Lacewood	5.5f	1:06 4/5	R. T. Wilson
1926	John J. Williams	5.5f	1:07	H. C. Fisher
1927	Sunchen	5.5f	1:07	W. S. Kilmer
1928	Crystal Broom	5.5f	1:06 4/5	Pineland Stable
1929	Dress Ship	5.5f	1:06 3/5	H. P. Whitney
1930	Porternesia	5.5f	1:09	F. J. Buchanan
1931	Towee	5.5f	1:06	Mrs. C. M. Amory

1932	Poppyman	5.5f	1:06 2/5	Mrs. J. H. Whitney
1933	High Glee	5.5f	1:06 3/5	C. V. Whitney
1934	Uppermost	5.5f	1:06 1/5	M. L. Schwartz
1935	Ned Reigh	5.5f	1:07 3/5	W. S. Kilmer
1936	Juliet W.	5.5f	1:06 3/5	B. Lissberger
1937	Wise Mentor	5.5f	1:06 2/5	H. W. Jackson
1938	Highscope	5.5f	1:06 1/5	G. D. Widener
1954	Sound Barrier	5.5f	1:05 2/5	E. M. O'Brien
1955	Reneged	5.5f	1:05	Woodley Lane Fm.

NOTE: In 1929, Martis finished first, but ran under the name of Cowlitz. Dress Ship finished second, and Mr. Whitney protested the situation. The stewards later disqualified the first-place horse and Dress Ship was declared the winner. The Troy was not run from 1939 to 1953

UNITED STATES HOTEL STAKES

1901	Masterman	5.5f	1:08	A. Belmont
1902	Skilful	5.5f	1:06 4/5	C. R. Ellison
1903	Montreson	5.5f	1:12	R. T. Wilson
1904	Woodsaw	5.5f	1:09	S. Paget
1905	Burgomaster	6f	1:13 4/5	H. P. Whitney
1906	De Mund	6f	1:14	P. Rainey
1907	Restigouche	6f	1:15	J. R. Keene
1908	Hilarious	6f	1:15	J. R. Keene
1909	Grasmere	6f	1:14 4/5	J. R. Keene
1910	Naushon	6f	1:14	R. T. Wilson

THE SARATOGA ASSOCIATION
FOR THE IMPROVEMENT OF THE BREED OF HORSES
6 AND 8 EAST 46TH STREET
NEW YORK

1913	Old Rosebud	6f	1:13 2/5	H. C. Applegate
1914	Garbage	6f	1:12 2/5	E. B. Cassatt
1915	Dominant	6f	1:13 2/5	L. S. Thompson
1916	Deer Trap	6f	1:14	A. Belmont
1917	Papp	6f	1:14 2/5	G. W. Loft
1918	Billy Kelly	6f	1:12 2/5	W. F. Polson
1919	Man o' War	6f	1:12 2/5	Glen Riddle Farm
1920	Nancy Lee	6f	1:11 4/5	P. A. Clark
1921	Morvich	6f	1:11 1/5	B. Block
1922	Martingale	6f	1:15	J. S. Cosden
1923	St. James	6f	1:12 3/5	G. D. Widener
1924	Sunny Man	6f	1:13	W. S. Kilmer
1925	Pompey	6f	1:16 3/5	Shoshone Stable
1926	Scapa Flow	6f	1:14 2/5	W. M. Jeffords
1927	Nassak	6f	1:12 2/5	Rancocas Stable
1928	Comstockery	6f	1:13	Greentree Stable
1929	Caruso	6f	1:12	W. R. Coe
1930	Jamestown	6f	1:11 3/5	G. D. Widener
1931	Morfair	6f	1:11 4/5	V. Emanuel
1932	Ladysman	6f	1:12 3/5	W. R. Coe
1933	Red Wagon	6f	1:14	Sagamore Stable
1934	Balladier	6f	1:13	E. R. Bradley
1935	Postage Due	6f	1:13 1/5	A. G. Vanderbilt
1936	Reaping Reward	6f	1:12 3/5	Milky Way Farm
1937	Chaps	6f	1:14 3/5	A. Untermyer
1938	El Chico	6f	1:13 1/5	W. Ziegler Jr.
1939	Flight Command	6f	1:13 2/5	C. V. Whitney
1940	Attention	6f	1:11 4/5	Mrs. P. Corning

1941	Buster	6f	1:12 2/5	J. H. Whitney
1942	Devil's Thumb	6f	1:12 1/5	W. E. Boeing
1943	Boy Knight	6f	1:13 1/5	C. Oglebay
1944	Pavot	6f	1:12 1/5	W.M. Jeffords
1945	Air Hero	6f	1:10 2/5	C. Oglebay
1946	I Will	6f	1:13	J. Paley
1947	My Request	6f	1:11 3/5	B. F. Whitaker
1948	The Admiral	6f	1:13 4/5	O. Phipps
1949	More Sun	6f	1:12	Brookmeade Stable
1950	Northern Star	6f	1:13	Mrs. E. D. Weir
1951	Jet Master	6f	1:12 1/5	Marlboro Stud
1952	Tahitian King	6f	1:12 4/5	B. F. Whitaker
1953	Wise Pop	6f	1:12 4/5	Mrs. C. Johannsen Jr.
1954	Summer Tan	6f	1:12 3/5	Mrs. R.A. Firestone
1955	Career Boy	6f	1:12 2/5	C. V. Whitney

WHITNEY STAKES

1928	Black Maria	10f	2:06	W. R. Coe
1929	Bateau	10f	2:09 2/5	W. M. Jeffords
1930	Whichone	10f	2:04	H. P. Whitney
1931	St. Brideaux	10f	2:05	Greentree Stable
1932	Equipoise	10f	2:05 3/5	C. V. Whitney
1933	Caesars Ghost	10f	2:10 4/5	Brookmeade Stable
1934	Discovery	10f	2:07 4/5	A. G. Vanderbilt
1935	Discovery	10f	2:04 3/5	A. G. Vanderbilt
1936	Discovery	10f	2:06 4/5	A. G. Vanderbilt
1937	Esposa	10f	2:05 1/5	W. Ziegler Jr.

1938	War Admiral	10f	2:03 4/5	Glen Riddle Farm
1939	Eight Thirty	10f	2:06 1/5	G. D. Widener
1940	Challedon	10f	2:03 1/5	W. L. Brann
1941	Fenelon	10f	2:06 2/5	Belair Stud
1942	Swing and Sway	10f	2:05 2/5	Greentree Stable
1943	Bolingbroke	10f	2:02	T. Martin
1944	Devil Diver	10f	2:02	Greentree Stable
1945	Trymenow	10f	2:02 1/5	W. M. Jeffords
1946	Stymie	10f	2:07 2/5	Mrs. E. D. Jacobs
1947	Rico Monte	10f	2:02 3/5	A. Hanger
1948	Gallorette	10f	2:05 1/5	W. L. Brann
1949	Round View	10f	2:03 1/5	Sanford Stud
1950	Piet	10f	2:06 3/5	P. A. Markey
1951	One Hitter	10f	2:05	Greentree Stable
1952	Counterpoint	10f	2:05 3/5	C. V. Whitney
1953	Tom Fool	10f	2:05 2/5	Greentree Stable
1954	Social Outcast	10f	2:04 2/5	A. G. Vanderbilt
1955	First Aid	9f	1:51 3/5	Brookmeade Stable

NOTE: The Whitney Handicap honors a great family of thoroughbred racing, one whose legacy is also of continuing support of civic causes in numerous communities.

WILSON HANDICAP

1930	Battleship Gray	8f	1:38 3/5	Glen Riddle Farm
1931	Blind Bowboy	8f	1:38	E. R. Bradley
1932	Equipoise	8f	1:38 1/5	C. V. Whitney

THE SARATOGA ASSOCIATION
FOR THE IMPROVEMENT OF THE BREED OF HORSES
6 AND 8 EAST 46TH STREET
NEW YORK

1933	Equipoise	8f	1:39	C. V. Whitney
1934	Observant	8f	1:37 3/5	M. L. Schwartz
1935	Discovery	8f	1:37 1/5	A. G. Vanderbilt
1936	Discovery	8f	1:38 4/5	A. G. Vanderbilt
1937	Esposa	8f	1:38 2/5	W. Ziegler Jr.
1938	War Admiral	8f	1:39 2/5	Glen Riddle Farm
1939	Eight Thirty	8f	1:37	G. D. Widener
1940	Eight Thirty	8f	1:39 1/5	G. D. Widener
1941	Parasang	8f	1:38 4/5	C. V. Whitney
1942	Apache	8f	1:37	Belair Stud
1943	Shut Out	8f	1:36 2/5	Greentree Stable
1944	Devil Diver	8f	1:36 1/5	Greentree Stable
1945	Brownie	8f	1:37	J. B. Yheall
1946	Pavot	8f	1:36 3/5	W. H. Jeffords
1947	Gallorette	8f	1:35 2/5	W. L. Brann
1948	Gallorette	8f	1:38 2/5	W. L. Brann
1949	Manyunk	8f	1:38 1/5	H. W. Collins
1950	Capot	8f	1:38 2/5	Greentree Stable
1951	Hall of Fame	8f	1:37 3/5	Greentree Stable
1952	Tom Fool	8f	1:39 2/5	Greentree Stable
1953	Tom Fool	8f	1:37 1/5	Greentree Stable
1954	First Glance	6f	1:11 3/5	A. G. Vanderbilt
1955	Mr. Turf	6f	1:11 3/5	J. J. Amiel

NOTE: The Wilson was named in honor of Richard T. Wilson, who was a member of the William C. Whitney syndicate that purchased Saratoga Race Course from Gottfried Walbaum in 1900. He later served as president of the Saratoga Association.

Appendix D
CHRONOLOGY OF NOTEWORTHY EVENTS

August 5, 1901   Opening day. The "Whitney Revival" of Saratoga Race Course begins under the leadership of Saratoga Association president William C. Whitney.

February 2, 1904   Death of William C. Whitney in New York City.

August 31, 1910   Final day of racing before a two-year blackout in 1911-1912. Novelty wins the Futurity Stakes, which was moved to Saratoga from Sheepshead Bay.

February 13, 1913   Death of Stephen Sanford.

August 2, 1913   Racing returns to Saratoga following the blackout.

August 23, 1913	The Sanford Memorial Stakes is inaugurated at Saratoga.
August 8, 1914	Regret wins the Saratoga Special in her career debut. She next won the Sanford Memorial on August 15 and the Hopeful Stakes on August 22 to complete her two-year-old season. In her next start, May 8, 1915, she became the first filly to win the Kentucky Derby.
August 13, 1919	Man o' War finishes second to Upset in the Sanford Memorial, his only loss in a career of 21 races.
August 30, 1919	Exterminator wins the first of four consecutive editions of the Saratoga Cup. The third, in 1921, was a walkover.
August 2, 1920	Sir Barton sets a track record of 2:01 4/5 in the Saratoga Handicap at 1 ¼ miles. The record was equaled by Man o' War in the Travers Stakes on August 21.

August 10, 1923	No racing due to the death of United States President Harding.
August 11, 1928	The Whitney Special, later called the Whitney Handicap and Whitney Stakes, is inaugurated.
December 29, 1929	Saratoga Association president Richard T. Wilson dies in New York City.
August 16, 1930	Gallant Fox is upset by Jim Dandy in the Travers Stakes.
August 25, 1934	Discovery wins the first of three consecutive editions of the Whitney, repeating in 1935 and 1936.
July 29, 1936	Maedic wins the Flash Stakes on opening day, the first of five stakes wins by the two-year-old that season. The others were the Saratoga Sales, Sanford, Grand Union Hotel, and Hopeful stakes.

THE SARATOGA ASSOCIATION
FOR THE IMPROVEMENT OF THE BREED OF HORSES
6 AND 8 EAST 46TH STREET
NEW YORK

July 7, 1938	Saratoga Association president George Bull resists the proposed match race between War Admiral and Seabiscuit for the upcoming meet. It took place on November 1, 1938 at Pimlico and was won by Seabiscuit.
July 29, 1940	Pari-mutuel wagering with the tote machines begins at Saratoga on opening day.
August 1, 1942	Devil's Thumb wins the United States Hotel, the first of five stakes that year. The others were the Saratoga Sales, Sanford, Grand Union Hotel and Hopeful stakes. He was second in the Flash Stakes on opening day, July 27.
August 29, 1942	Final day of racing at Saratoga before the transfer of dates to Belmont Park for 1943, 1944, and 1945.
August 5, 1946	Racing returns to Saratoga.

THE SARATOGA ASSOCIATION
FOR THE IMPROVEMENT OF THE BREED OF HORSES
6 AND 8 EAST 46TH STREET
NEW YORK

August 6, 1951 The National Museum of Racing opens, with its exhibits at the Canfield Casino in Congress Park, Saratoga Springs.

April 29, 1955 New York Governor Averell Harriman signs legislation creating the Greater New York Association. Later that year, the GNYA acquired the stock of the Saratoga Association.

THE SARATOGA ASSOCIATION
FOR THE IMPROVEMENT OF THE BREED OF HORSES
6 AND 8 EAST 46TH STREET
NEW YORK

NOTES

1. GIANTS OF THE YOUNG CENTURY 1901-1910

1. *New York Times,* 4 August 1901.

2. *Saratogian,* 19 November 1901.

3. *Saratogian,* 9 July 1906.

4. *Saratogian,* 25 August 1905.

5. William C. Whitney, *The Whitney Stud* (New York: Press of Styles and Cash, 1902), xxxvii.

6. National Turf Writers Association, comp. *Horses in the National Museum of Racing Hall of Fame,* Saratoga Springs, NY: National Museum of Racing, p. 123, n.d.

7. "A Century of Champions," *The Blood Horse* CXIII, no. 6 (7 February 1987): 1060.

8. *Saratogian,* 22 July 1905.

9. *The Blood Horse,* 7 February 1987, 1060.

10. *Saratogian,* 31 July 1908.

NOTES

2. BLACKOUT 1911-1912

1. *Goodwin's Turf Guide* (New York: Goodwin Bros., 1908), 124.

2. *Saratogian,* 26 August 1908.

3. *New York Times,* 12 August 1908.

4. *The American Racing Manual 2008* (New York: Daily Racing Form Press, 2008), 957.

5. *The American Racing Manual 2008* (New York: Daily Racing Form Press, 2008), 800.

6. *Schenectady Evening Star,* 14 August 1911.

7. *Saratogian,* 27 July 1911.

8. *New York Times,* 14 October 1912.

NOTES

3. RESTORATION AND A GOLDEN AGE OF RACING 1913-1939

1. *Saratogian,* 14 August 1919.

2. *Champions, 1894-2010* (New York, NY: Daily Racing Form Press, 2011), 34.

3. *New York Times,* 27 August 1916.

4. *Thoroughbred Times,* 12 July 2003, 22.

5. *Saratogian,* 19 September 1932.

6. *New York Times,* 17 August 1940.

7. *New York Times,* 29 January 1925.

8. *Saratogian,* 30 December 1929.

9. *New York Times,* 11 August 1935.

10. *New York Times,* 8 July 1938.

NOTES

4. PARI-MUTUELS ARRIVE AND WORLD WAR II 1940-1945

1. Harry D. Snyder, interview by the author, 3 October 2007.

5. RETURN TO SARATOGA AND A NEW ORDER FOR THE FUTURE

1. Ernie Lloyd, interview by the author, 5 June 2007.

2. John Mangona, interview by the author, 14 November 2007.

3. Bowen, Edward L., *Legacies of the Turf – A Century of Great Thoroughbred Breeders,* vol. 1, Eclipse Press, Lexington, KY, 2003, 73.

4. *The American Racing Manual* (New York: Daily Racing Form 1946-1955), n.p.

5. *Legislative Annual 1955* (New York: New York State Legislative Service, 1955), 142-145.

6. Memorandum, 11 February 1955, New York State Library.

7. Ashley Trimble Cole to Governor Harriman, 4 April 1955, New York State Library.

THE SARATOGA ASSOCIATION
FOR THE IMPROVEMENT OF THE BREED OF HORSES
6 AND 8 EAST 46TH STREET
NEW YORK

NOTES

8. Memorandum, 11 April 1955, New York State Library.

9. George M. Braglani, Commissioner of Taxation and Finance, to Governor Averell Harriman, 12 April 1955, New York State Library.

10. A. Fairfield Dana to Daniel Gutman, 14 April 1955, New York State Library.

11. Telegram by Max Hirsch, 1955, New York State Library.

12. Isidor Bieber to Daniel Gutman, 25 April 1955, New York State Library.

13. Jerome Fendrick to Daniel Gutman, 25 April 1955, New York State Library.

14. Cyrus Jullien to Governor Averell Harriman, 20 April 1955, New York State Library.

15. Greater New York Association to stockholders of the Saratoga Association for the Improvement of the Breed, 25 July 1955, New York State Library.

16. *New York Times*, 11 April 1958.

THE SARATOGA ASSOCIATION
FOR THE IMPROVEMENT OF THE BREED OF HORSES
6 AND 8 EAST 46TH STREET
NEW YORK

SELECTED BIBLIOGRAPHY

BOOKS

The American Racing Manual 1945-2010. New York: Daily Racing Form, 1945-2010.

Bowen, Edward L. *Legacies of the Turf – A Century of Great Thoroughbred Breeders. Vol. 1*. Lexington, KY: Blood-Horse Publications, 2003.

------ *Legacies of the Turf – A Century of Great Thoroughbred Breeders. Vol. 2*. Lexington, KY: Blood Horse Publications 2004.

------*Matriarchs – Great Mares of the 20th Century*. Lexington, KY: The Blood-Horse, 1999.

------ *Matriarchs – Volume II: More Great Mares of Modern Times*. Lexington, KY: The Blood-Horse, 2008.

Britten, Evelyn Barrett. *Chronicles of Saratoga*. Saratoga Springs, NY: Bradshaw Printing Co., 1947.

Champions 1894-2010. New York, NY: Daily Racing Form Press, 2011.

The Great Ones. Lexington, KY: The Blood-Horse, 1970.

Hildebrandt, Louis F. Jr. *Hurricana – Thoroughbred Dynasty,*

THE SARATOGA ASSOCIATION
FOR THE IMPROVEMENT OF THE BREED OF HORSES
6 AND 8 EAST 46TH STREET
NEW YORK

Amsterdam Landmark: A Sanford Legacy Revisited. Troy, NY: The Troy Book Makers, 2009.

Hotaling, Edward. *They're Off – Horse Racing at Saratoga.* Syracuse, NY: Syracuse University Press, 1995.

The Jockey Club's Illustrated History of Thoroughbred Racing in America. New York: Little Brown and Company, 1974.

National Turf Writers Association, comp. *Horses in the National Museum of Racing and Hall of Fame.* Saratoga Springs, NY: National Museum of Racing.

Robertson, William H.P. *The History of Thoroughbred Racing in America.* Inglewood Cliffs, NJ: Prentice-Hall Inc., 1964.

Thoroughbred Champions: Top 100 Racehorses of the 20th Century. Lexington, KY: The Blood-Horse, Inc., 1999.

Whitney, W.C. *The Whitney Stud.* New York: Press of Styles and Cash, 1902.

ANNUAL PUBLICATIONS AND CALENDARS

Goodwin's Turf Guide 1908. New York: Goodwin Bros., 1908.

Legislative Annual 1955. New York: New York State Legislative Service, 1955.

PERIODICALS

"A Century of Champions." *The Blood-Horse*, 7 February 1987.

Thoroughbred Times, 12 July 2003.

NEWSPAPERS

New York Times 1901-1955.

Saratogian (Saratoga Springs, New York), 1901-1955.

THE SARATOGA ASSOCIATION
FOR THE IMPROVEMENT OF THE BREED OF HORSES
6 AND 8 EAST 46TH STREET
NEW YORK

THE SARATOGA ASSOCIATION
FOR THE IMPROVEMENT OF THE BREED OF HORSES
6 AND 8 EAST 46TH STREET
NEW YORK

ACKNOWLEDGEMENTS AND CREDITS

I am thankful to all who provided help and support for this book.

Gale Y. Brinkman is the editor of this work, as she was for my first book, *Foundations of Fame.* Her professional guidance shaped the organization and presentation of both.

The cover art is by Anthony P. Farone, Jr., of Saratoga Springs. I asked Anthony to imagine a scene that captures the style of Saratoga Race Course circa 1930, as it would look if viewed by someone on Union Avenue.

I am lucky to have the services of talented proofreaders. My wife Gail, and Richard Hamilton, who served as a steward at New York Racing Association tracks and as a Media Director at the National Museum of Racing and Hall of Fame, both made sharp observations and corrections for this book. Allan Carter, historian at the Museum and a treasured friend of racing, and former teachers Elinor Riter and Laurence Onody were also helpful as proofreaders, making numerous suggestions that were incorporated in the text.

Steve Bochnak, long a member of the New York State Assembly

THE SARATOGA ASSOCIATION
FOR THE IMPROVEMENT OF THE BREED OF HORSES
6 AND 8 EAST 46TH STREET
NEW YORK

Program and Counsel Staff, is another proofreader who made important notes on this work, especially the section in Chapter 5 sub-titled "A New Order for New York Racing." It covers the legislation that created the New York Racing Association. So, too, was the help with this section provided by Gerard J. McKeon, who served as President of the New York Racing Association from 1982-1994. His knowledge of the creation of the New York Racing Association, and the components and impact of the franchise law, is much appreciated and undoubtedly helps the reader understand a complex period.

Diana Burke, of Saratoga Springs, provided information about her relatives Thomas and Anne Clare, in whose honor the Clare Court section of the main track was named. Mr. and Mrs. Clare both served as track superintendents at Saratoga Race Course.

Saratoga Springs attorney Harry D. Snyder, a lifelong fan of Saratoga thoroughbred racing and a contributor in many ways, guided me through the evolution of the New York law in 1957 that guaranteed racing dates for the track during a time of worry about its future.

I also thank Brien Bouyea, Communications Coordinator for the National Museum of Racing and Hall of Fame, for his help in locating several photos and for his views in general on the book. The

THE SARATOGA ASSOCIATION
FOR THE IMPROVEMENT OF THE BREED OF HORSES
6 AND 8 EAST 46TH STREET
NEW YORK

photos of racing greats Regret, on page 35, Discovery, on page 52, and Tom Fool, on page 89 are courtesy of the National Museum of Racing.

This book, as well as *Foundations of Fame*, owes a great deal to the skill of Mark and Kimberly Sutton of Advantage Press in Saratoga Springs. From start to finish, they offered guidance as each book was being written.

Photographer Russell G. Melton lent his advice and creativity on several occasions. He is responsible for three photographs on these pages. They are the Stephen Sanford mausoleum and Sanford family burial plots on page 10, the view of Clare Court on page 59, and the view of the Oklahoma Training Track on page 107.

The photo on page 27, of Fort Erie Race Track in Ontario, is reproduced from *A Centennial Celebration,* a publication from 1997 honoring the 100th anniversary of the track. It appears on page four of that publication and was taken on opening day, June 16, 1897. It was provided to the author from the archives of the Canadian Horse Racing Hall of Fame with the assistance of Louis E. Cauz, a renowned historian of the Queen's Plate and author of two books on his nation's great horse race.

The diagram of the betting rings on page 72 appears courtesy of Harry D. Snyder, and the photo of Thomas and Anne Clare on

THE SARATOGA ASSOCIATION
FOR THE IMPROVEMENT OF THE BREED OF HORSES
6 AND 8 EAST 46TH STREET
NEW YORK

page 75 was taken by *The Daily News* of New York and is from the collection of Diana Burke.

Reproductions of the 1922 and 1955 programs of the Saratoga Association on pages 41 and 95, respectively, are from the collection of the author.

The emblem that appears throughout this book is a reproduction of a page of stationery of the Saratoga Association from 1917. The officers that year were president, Richard T. Wilson, vice-president, Harry Payne Whitney, and secretary-treasurer, Andrew Miller.